The Great Struggle

THE GREAT STRUGGLE

STRUGGLE

LABOR IN AMERICA

by Irving Werstein

CHARLES SCRIBNER'S SONS   New York

35-47

For those devoted men and women of the American Labor Movement who braved dangers and made sacrifices so that others might enjoy a better life

ACKNOWLEDGMENTS

The illustration on page 22 is taken from an original indenture paper in the collection of the Hingham Historical Society.

The illustrations on pages 26–27, 65, 84–85, 92–93 are reproduced from *Frank Leslie's Illustrated Newspaper*.

The illustrations on pages 96–97, 111, 125, 133 are reproduced from *Harper's Weekly* through the courtesy of the New-York Historical Society, as is the illustration on pages 52–53 from *Frank Leslie's Illustrated Newspaper*.

The illustration on page 105 is reproduced from *Puck*.

The illustrations on page 145 are reproduced from *Mill Town* by Bill Cahn, New York: Cameron & Kahn, 1954.

The illustration on pages 150–151 is reproduced from *Harper's Weekly*.

The illustration on page 165 is reproduced through the courtesy of the Photographic Division, Federal Art Project, WPA.

CONTENTS

Today in the United States labor unions and industry have a common meeting ground. Both are Big Business.

Out of a working force numbering some 70,000,000 about 17,000,000 men and women belong to a union. They pay staggering sums of money into union treasuries; and the unions have grown rich.

More than 50 labor unions operate large national offices in Washington, D.C., and many have erected modern office structures in the national capital at a total expenditure of over $30,000,000. The A.F. of L.-C.I.O. headquarters was built at an outlay of $4,000,000. The International Brotherhood of Teamsters building cost $5,000,000. The Bakers and Confectionery Workers International Union put up an edifice worth $6,000,000. Not many corporations can boast such valuable real estate.

The International Ladies' Garment Workers and the Amalgamated Clothing Workers have built and manage large apartment house developments. Unions run banks, health centers, hospitals, summer resorts, camps and various other enterprises. Membership in a union often entitles a worker to such privileges as buying household goods, medicines, clothing and even a car at substantial discounts in the union-managed cooperative store.

Since World War II a new era has blossomed between

11

management and labor. In garment, auto, steel and other industries, the unions no longer merely seek wage increases or improved working conditions—these have already been achieved. Instead, negotiations revolve around guaranteed annual wages, profit sharing, employer contributions to welfare funds, sick pay and other benefits.

This does not mean that *all* unions have attained *all* labor's demands. The Era of Good Feeling in industry is fragile; strikes occur from time to time but are seldom marked by the violence of the old days.

New and stirring issues face labor unions in the years immediately ahead. Negroes and Puerto Ricans, long discriminated against in certain unions, now want equality and the right to union membership if qualified to do the work. The record of some unions on racial bias is not good. However, steps have been taken to alleviate these abuses, and as a labor expert predicted, "A new day is dawning when no man will be barred from belonging to a union because of race, creed, or his political beliefs . . ."

Sometimes unions are run by venal men who embezzle funds. They are infiltrated by criminal elements, hoodlums, and racketeers. But these are flaws in a splendid tapestry; most union leaders are strong, incorruptible men who believe in their cause.

Even in these days of affluent unionism, organizers still go out into the field bringing the union to migratory workers, workers in sweatshops, the hordes of unorganized workers still toiling for minimal wages under poor conditions. While many women workers have attained "equal pay for equal work" in factories and shops, thousands still receive lower pay than men on the same job.

And just ahead lies the knottiest problem of all for trade unionists—the coming of a new industrial revolution where the increasing use of automation will make obsolete an ever-growing number of jobs. Unions are already planning to retrain their members for different work. Despite tall buildings, high-powered executives, the outward trappings of wealth, labor unions are no stronger than the working class that created them.

In the beginning there was struggle. . . .

If it had not been for this thing, I might have lived out my life talking on street corners to scorning men. I might have died, unmarked, unknown, a failure. Now we are not a failure. This is our career and our triumph. Never in our full life could we hope to do such work for tolerance, for justice, for man's understanding of man, as now we do by accident. Our words—our pains—nothing! The taking of our lives—the lives of a good shoemaker and a poor fish-peddler—all! The last moment belongs to us—that agony is our triumph!

Bartolomeo Vanzetti—On the eve of
his execution, August 22, 1927.

Work and Pray,
Live on hay,
You'll get pie
In the sky,
When you die!

I.W.W. Song

"I can hire one half of the working class to kill the other half."
Jay Gould, Railroad Magnate.

The Planting Time

1786–1865

New York City was startled on a spring day in 1786 by an unusual event. The journeymen printers of that city had banded together to ask their employers for a $1 daily wage. When this demand was rejected, the printers walked off their jobs to bring on America's first organized strike, called a "turnout" in the slang of that day.

The workers' tactics forced the employers to give in. Triumphant journeymen printers jubilantly returned to work; they had gained a tremendous victory and the news of it spread from city to city.

A wave of "turnouts" swept the Eastern seaboard. Journeymen tailors, weavers, bakers, gunsmiths, upholsterers, wigmakers and coppersmiths, workers in every craft, downed tools for higher pay. The strikers paraded outside places of employment, carrying signs and shouting their demands. These primitive picket lines were known as "tramping committees."

But because the workers had united only temporarily for the purpose of obtaining more money, the initial drift toward trade unionism did not last long. Once the objective had been achieved, the journeymen's loosely knit organization simply faded away. The men consequently learned a painful lesson. No sooner had fledgling unions been dissolved than bosses promptly withdrew pay raises and the journeymen had to start all over again.

"Only through organization can we hold our gains and better our conditions . . ." a journeyman printer noted.

The American workingman had been moving toward that conclusion for more than a century, ever since colonists first planted roots in the New World. Skilled workers were needed from the very outset. In 1609, Captain John Smith, a founder of the Jamestown colony in Virginia, wrote the London Company which had financed the expedition that established the settlement. "When you send again, I entreat you rather send but thirty carpenters, husbandmen, gardeners, fishermen, masons and diggers of tree roots, well provided, than a thousand such as we have . . ."

Smith's request stemmed from the bitter experiences of the original Jamestown settlers. Much suffering could have been avoided had there been men among them who knew how to use axe, saw and hammer. Instead, the colonists consisted of gentlemen adventurers, swashbuckling soldiers or pampered idlers. Such men were destined to perish in the wilderness.

As more colonies opened on America's eastern shore, the founding companies sought as settlers men who could put up houses and forts; men able to fell trees, clear land, build boats, tan leather and till fields. Good carpenters or stonemasons who "lived by the sweat of their brows" were worth more than all the elegant dandies of London society.

America held untapped riches; no man could reckon the potentials of the New World's resources. The great continent had room for cities, towns and villages. There beckoned the prospect of seaports teeming with commerce to overshadow ages-old European trade centers and markets. But the New World was only a promise. America's trackless forests and boundless spaces had to be conquered before the new land could be made livable. America offered hope and room to grow. It was a bright promise to the masses of the Old World who saw only despair and bleakness stretching before them. In England and on the Continent, men roamed the streets of every city seeking work. A series of wars had laid waste farming regions and blighted crops; hunger followed in the wars' wake.

The common man, entrapped in misery, facing starvation, seemed at a dead end. Writers of the time predicted Europe's doom; overpopulation was causing a food shortage and soon there would not be enough to eat.

"Only pestilences and plagues; wars and famines; or similar great catastrophes which will wipe out thousands upon thousands can save us from slow death by starvation . . ." a gloomy Englishman prophesied.

Among the uprooted who wandered aimlessly in search of a job were innumerable skilled workers, the very ones so badly needed in America. Conditions worsened during the early years of the eighteenth century. In 1715 alone, almost 2,000,000 Frenchmen died of malnutrition.

The people of Europe grew desperate; rumblings of discontent growled across the Continent and the British Isles. Kings' ministers heard these sounds and recognized their portent. Something had to be done; the plight of the masses must be relieved or else all Europe might erupt in revolution.

Solving the Old World's problem proved to be fairly simple. Wealthy men were presented by their governments with tremendous tracts in America. The officials then said, in effect, "You now have land. Take the starving wretches who crowd our cities and transport them to America. There, do with them as you like . . ."

The landowners could carve out personal empires for them-

indenture paper of a fifteen-year-old English boy, 1715

selves in America—they lacked only subjects. These were not difficult to find. Hungry men could easily be persuaded to pull up stakes and with their wives and children make a new start in America.

The landlords sent out agents among the people to sign up prospective settlers. Workers responded by the scores and the hundreds. Since most had no money, shipmasters devised a scheme which required no cash payment for passage from the prospective immigrants.

Vessels plying the Atlantic carried back timber, furs, tobacco and rum from America. They often made the return voyage to the colonies without much cargo and had space in their holds. The wily captains reasoned that they could use the empty holds to haul human beings, cramming their ships with men, women and children bound for America.

The penniless voyager financed his trip by signing a contract, called an indenture, with the ship's captain; the worker bound himself to labor for a fixed number of years, usually five, turning over to the shipmaster all his earnings during that period as payment for expenses incurred on the journey.

Not even this unfair practice could deter the downtrodden Europeans from embarking for the New World where they believed "fertile soil awaited the plow . . . and land was for the asking . . . In this world, the woods were so thick that one could not pass through them . . . the forests abounded with game and the rivers with fish . . . In this New World, hunger was unknown and there was no war, no oppression . . ."

This was the dream.

Reality had another face; a cruel and harsh one. A remorseless face without pity or compassion.

The voyage itself was a nightmare. Hapless passengers were crammed into ill-ventilated holds. Their food crawled with maggots and drinking water was foul. Many immigrants died en route. Their corpses were unceremoniously dumped overboard. The ships in which they sailed were often unseaworthy hulks; the number of ships that went down in Atlantic storms or the lives lost by drowning were unrecorded.

Gaunt survivors of the ghastly journey staggered ashore "more dead than alive," according to one observer, and soon learned America was no Eden.

The ship captains who held the original indenture papers never meant to wait five years for their money. Instead, they sold the bondsmen like so many sheep, to the highest bidder. Sales of indentured immigrants were held as the ship docked and crowds gathered for the auction which was advertised in handbills, posters and by town criers.

There was spirited bidding for the blacksmiths, carpenters, weavers, shoemakers, coopers, silversmiths and other craftsmen in the cargo. Once these unfortunates had been sold, they became virtual slaves under the law. Instead of finding freedom in the New World, they met with cruel oppression, harsher than that from which they had fled.

The lot of the so-called white slaves was described by the historian, John Bach McMasters, in these words:

"They were worked hard, were dressed in the cast-off clothes of their owners and might be flogged as often as the master thought necessary. If a 'white slave' ran away . . . two days might be added to his time of service for each day he was absent. Fathers, mothers and children could be sold to different buyers . . . Such remnants of cargoes as could not find purchasers at the auction . . . were bought in lots of 50 or more by a class of speculators known as 'soul drivers' . . . who led them through the country like so many cattle and sold them for what they could bring . . ."

The indentured person was further bound by restrictive measures. He could not marry without consent of his master or mistress and any violation of this rule meant a year's additional servitude.

Side by side with white bondage grew another form of slavery. On a sunny day in August of 1619, a Dutch ship, the "Treasurer," dropped anchor off Jamestown, Virginia. The arrival of any ship was an exciting event for the settlers, but the "Treasurer" caused more than the usual commotion. Her captain had brought twenty strong Negroes whom he offered for sale as field hands. The tobacco planters, needing manpower, quickly bought the Negroes, and on that day the enslavement of black men set its roots in American soil. Eventually it would bear evil fruit.

At first Negro slavery was practiced throughout all the colonies on the Atlantic seaboard, but it did not last long in New England and other northern provinces. In the words of one historian: "This type of slavery did not pay on small farms as were found in New England . . . it was quickly made clear that Africans were not adaptable for industry and commerce . . . hence, economics and not scruples ended Negro slavery in the north . . ."

Even in the South, slavery failed to flourish immediately. Not until 1630 did a second slave ship, the "Fortune," come to Virginia with more Negroes who were sold for "85 barrels of rum and 5 barrels of tobacco."

The slave trade was destined to be unprofitable for many years. By 1635 there were only 26 Negro slaves in all Virginia.

Negro slaves picking cotton, sketched by A. R. Waud

But by 1860, more than 4,000,000 Negro slaves toiled in the south. The great flood of African slaves came at the end of the eighteenth century, when Eli Whitney invented the cotton gin. Until then, cotton had been a relatively unprofitable crop because of difficulties in picking the ripened bolls.

Whitney's machine simplified the task and planters who had been reluctant to grow cotton now found they could make money raising it. Soon huge cotton plantations covered the South and sparked an insatiable demand for African slaves to work them; the blacks, accustomed to tropical climes, fared far better under southern sun than did whites.

By the start of the nineteenth century, slave traders were among America's wealthiest men. Ship captains, engaged in the ugly business of carrying Negroes from Africa and selling them in America, made fortunes on a few voyages. Negro slaves had worked in tobacco fields and rice paddies since 1619, but the need for them on cotton plantations quickly outstripped the supply. At slave auctions planters bid eagerly, paying $400 or more for a sturdy field hand.

A Negro slave owned by the same master as a white one, was often treated far better. The Negro was a master's permanent property while the white remained his for only five years or so. Obviously, the owner would take greater care of his Negro. He wanted the black man to last a long time, but was little concerned with the well-being of his white chattel, especially as the indenture term drew to a close.

Throughout the eighteenth century, white slavery flourished in every colony; indentured bondsmen were auctioned in Philadelphia, Boston and New York as well as Jamestown, Charleston and St. Augustine. One writer claimed that more than half the working people in the colonies were indentured servants required to labor at least five years.

Collecting and shipping white slaves to America became a lucrative business. Shipmasters hired men known as "crimps" to round up the immigrants. The crimps, often criminals, used guile, trickery and force to get recruits for whom they were paid by the head. Many a workman was waylaid, knocked senseless and carried aboard a vessel heading for America. Prisons were emptied of "vagrants, debtors and beggars." In some cities, orphan children were shipped out to America where they toiled as household servants.

28

The American colonies grew and prospered on the labor of slaves—black and white. For the latter, there glimmered, at last, the hope of eventual freedom when terms of bondage came to an end, but as the slave trade expanded, Negroes faced a barren vista of eternal enslavement, never to live without fetters, never to enjoy a free man's dignity and pride.

For eight grim years, 1775–1783, the colonies were torn by the American Revolution. Out of the blood and pain of that struggle the United States was born. No one in the colonies was untouched by the war; every man's life was altered. Many who fought had known the degradation of indentured slavery. Some had gained freedom after working out their bondage; some had been born free, although their fathers had come to America as bondsmen.

During the decades before the Revolution, thousands of white slaves had finished their periods of indenture. With that grueling time ended, these craftsmen either went to work for themselves or took paid employment.

Any man adept at his trade had no difficulty finding a job. Some workers set up small shops to supply the demands of the local population. Although wealthy people chose to import clothing and furniture from Europe, the average citizen patronized local artisans.

Every town and city had its little shops, which were usually located in a workman's home. Shoemakers' hammers tapped from dawn to dusk; cabinetmakers' lathes whined far into the night; tailors' needles shuttled busily.

A master craftsman often owned not only his shop, but also a small plot of land near it. When business was slack, he tilled the land to raise food for his family. The masters were independent men, respected by all in the community. They lived modestly but well. Long hours at the bench meant nothing to them; each man took pride in his work; everything, from wigs to coaches, was made by hand.

The sign hanging above a shop door announced to a passerby the specialty of its proprietor. A wooden boot swaying in the wind marked the shop of a shoemaker; a pair of wooden shears indicated a tailor; each trade had its own symbol.

If the rush of orders became too great for the craftsman to handle alone, he hired an assistant known as a journeyman or mechanic, less skilled than the master and not yet ready to go into business for himself.

Journeymen were willing to put in many hours for modest wages in order to improve their skills. They worked beside the craftsman, preparing for the day when they would become masters in their own right. The relationship between master and journeyman was a good one. They jointly formed benefit societies to provide funds in case of sickness, accident or death.

Most shops also had apprentices—young boys bound out to a craftsman for five or six years to learn a trade. The master paid an apprentice no wages, but gave him food, clothing and shelter. The youths, in turn, performed the menial and irksome tasks connected with a particular craft. Gradually, an apprentice became a journeyman and eventually went on to be a master.

During the colonial period, this system proved satisfactory. The craftsmen were able to supply local markets and there was enough work for all. If a community had too many men engaged in the same trade, a worker had only to move on to a settlement where his services were needed. In this simple economy of supply and demand, the craftsman not only provided his own materials, but also did the work and fixed prices.

Soon after the Revolution, the country began spreading

out. By the 1780's America experienced tremendous changes. Thousands of settlers pushed west beyond the Alleghenies to new territories. The pioneers needed goods made in the East—everything from plowshares to shirts. Europe also became an expanding market for American-made products after wars between France and England disrupted normal trade channels.

With the rising market for manufactured goods, craftsmen could not produce sufficient quantities. The old way of working was outmoded, the day of personal association between consumer and craftsman ending. A local shoemaker or tailor, geared to supply his own clientele, could not keep up the pace called for by the enlarged market.

The economic structure underwent a drastic change. For the first time on the American scene a new character appeared. Known variously as jobber, distributor, middleman or merchant capitalist, he acted as the link between the local artisan and the outside market. The old order faded away. The craftsman was a free agent no more. His products were bought by merchant capitalists for distribution to the public; in addition, the middleman also became the artisan's prime supplier of raw materials.

Since the credo of merchant capitalists was "buy low, sell high," they snapped up the output of independent craftsmen at "wholesale" prices and sold at a large profit. The price paid to the craftsman was lower than he usually received from his own customers, but the jobbers kept him busy and he was relieved of the need to find a market.

Merchant capitalists bought wares of all sorts—furniture, spinning wheels, clocks, plows, shoes, clothing, spun cloths. They held them in warehouses until needed and made handsome sums by selling to retailers. Primarily interested in quantity, not quality, the middleman put up cash for huge stocks of products called "job lots."

Under the new system, the master craftsman actually worked for the merchant capitalist, and although busier than ever made less money on each item. Masters tried to overcome this contradiction by cutting costs. They lowered journeymen's salaries, or replaced the journeymen with low-paid apprentices. The working day was extended from "sunup to sundown"— 12 hours in the winter and 16 in the summer.

Cordiality in the workshop soon vanished. Journeymen grumbled over pay cuts and long hours. A Philadelphia shoemaker wrote, ". . . no matter how hard I work . . . I earn only eight and one-half dollars a week . . . and I am at the bench from five in the morning until sunset . . ."

Animosity developed between master and journeyman. The mutual benefit societies went out of existence. To take their place organizations for journeymen only were formed and these new groups did not limit their purpose to sickness or death funds. The journeymen banded together as protection against the abuses being heaped upon them by the masters.

The labor movement in the United States was emerging; the trade union was being born, sired by the discontent of workingmen caught in the changing economy. No man knew then the sacrifice, bloodshed and struggle that lay ahead in the ceaseless war between capital and labor, boss and worker.

When the floodtide of "turnouts" (or strikes) which broke in 1786 finally receded, workingmen began to cast about for the most suitable way to band together for their own protection. A number of attempts were made to start organizations but each failed until 1792 when the cordwainers (shoemakers) of Philadelphia established a permanent union with a constitution, dues, elected officers and regularly scheduled meetings. This was the first local trade union in the United States.

Two years later, the printers in New York City who had initiated the turnout set up a union. The movement gained momentum and by 1804 trade unions or "societies" existed in almost every kind of work. Dues were modest, usually a 50-cent initiation fee and monthly assessments of five to eight cents.

These societies kept their membership rolls secret because bosses made blacklists of society members and circulated the names throughout the trade to prevent unionists from getting jobs. However, the men remained undaunted. They swore never to work for less than the minimum union wage and to join a turnout when the majority voted for one.

Life was made unbearable for any union man who turned against his fellows and refused to take part in a strike. He was ostracized by former friends, cursed and reviled. A non-striker was called a "scab"; no man was more despised than he.

Union members tried to persuade everyone practicing a

34

craft in a particular locality to join their society. They were not always successful and violence sometimes exploded during a turnout when scabs and strikers clashed. Employers also hired men to act as strikebreakers; these were often underworld types handier with pistol, knife or blackjack than with the tools of a trade. Many gory battles flared between strikebreakers and strikers.

From the inception of unionism the members realized that work stoppages and strikes were their chief weapon when argument, logic and appeals failed. Special funds were set aside in the union treasury to provide money for men who joined a turnout and marched with the tramping committees.

Employers opposed unions with every means at their disposal. Newspapers usually sided with the employer in a strike and sought to influence the public against trade unions.

Early in the nineteenth century, during a strike by Boston journeymen carpenters demanding a 10-hour workday and a 50-cent per diem increase, a local paper ran an editorial on the turnout:

"We cannot believe this project to have originated with any of the faithful and industrious sons of New England . . . but are compelled to consider it an evil of foreign growth . . . and one which we pray will not take root in the favored soil of New England . . ."

The newspaper's readers denounced the striking carpenters as "foreign agitators." With public opinion against them the strikers lost heart and the strike ended in dismal failure.

But the employers found a more effective weapon to use on the unions—the courts. In March, 1806, eight Philadelphia cordwainers or shoemakers, were on trial. The charge against them, based on English common law, was "criminal conspiracy."

THE TRIAL

OF THE

BOOT & SHOEMAKERS

OF PHILADELPHIA,

ON AN INDICTMENT

FOR A COMBINATION AND CONSPIRACY

TO RAISE THEIR WAGES.

TAKEN IN SHORT-HAND,
BY THOMAS LLOYD.

PHILADELPHIA:

PRINTED BY B. GRAVES, NO. 40, NORTH FOURTH-STREET,
FOR T. LLOYD, AND B. GRAVES.

1806.

title-page of a pamphlet published in Philadelphia, 1806

Their crime was to have formed a union; their conspiracy, banding together to force a raise in wages. All Philadelphia followed the case with interest and its outcome was awaited across the whole country.

The jury found the workers were indeed guilty as charged. The judge ruled it illegal for workers to unite and refuse to work. The jury, made up of twelve businessmen, openly admitted bias against the accused cordwainers, but the verdict was upheld even on appeal to a higher court.

If workers formed a "society, association, union or club" with the purpose of increasing wages, that organization constituted a conspiracy, membership in it was outlawed, and anyone who joined was liable to criminal prosecution. As a result of the cordwainers' case, unions remained illegal in the United States until 1842 when Chief Justice Lemuel Shaw of the Massachusetts Supreme Court held that they were not "conspiracies" and therefore legal if formed for lawful purposes, such as gaining better working conditions and higher wages.

In the thirty-six years between the cordwainers' case and Judge Shaw's decision, workers continued to organize despite the ban on unions. There were numerous strikes—tailors walked out in Buffalo, ship carpenters in Philadelphia, cabinetmakers in Baltimore. New York City had strikes involving painters, stonecutters, masons, day laborers and glaziers. The turnouts were often violent. Men were maimed, beaten and sometimes jailed.

An outstanding exception to the pattern of violence came during 1842 in a strike by female weavers of a Pawtucket, Rhode Island, textile mill. The women struck for shorter hours and more pay. There was nothing unusual about these demands.

But the way the strikers conducted themselves attracted widespread attention.

Instead of resorting to noisy demonstrations, the strike, according to a newspaper reporter who covered it, went on ". . . without noise, without clamor, with barely a word spoken . . . the women stood outside the mill gate, hour after hour in almost total silence . . ." The tactic proved effective, and within a few days the women won the strike.

"We could have withstood a clamoring riotous mob . . . but that ghostlike silence was more than we could endure . . . and so we met their demands . . ." a spokesman for the mill-owners later said.

Thus, in one form or another, the struggle between worker and employer continued, growing ever sharper in the nineteenth century. The conditions in the late 1700's which had begun to eliminate the independent craftsman, by destroying the master-journeyman-apprentice relationship and creating the merchant capitalist, now effected still further changes.

By the first decade of the nineteenth century, the factory system of production made its appearance in American economic life. Merchant capitalists could not satisfy ever-enlarging markets with products supplied by the handwork of craftsmen. A speedier, less expensive system of production had to be utilized. The answer was found in a theory put forth some years earlier, by an economist named William Petty, who wrote:

"Cloth must be cheaper, when one worker cards, another spins, another weaves, another presses and packs, than when all the above operations are performed by the same hands . . ."

This method—the division of labor—appealed to merchant capitalists who opened large workrooms, hired workers and started making a variety of products. The manufacturing operation was broken down into several steps and each workman was given a specific task to do. He repeated the process over and over, merely performing his small part in producing the whole. The technique proved highly satisfactory. Production was speeded up; unskilled, low-paid workers, trained to do a single job, replaced higher-priced craftsmen.

Machines were invented for some operations and the groundwork laid for the modern factory system. In fact, as early as 1789, an Englishman, Samuel Slater, had built a water-power driven textile mill in Rhode Island.

Not until the War of 1812, however, when the supply of manufactured goods from Great Britain was cut off, would factories mushroom in the United States. The first plants were textile mills located along the streams and falls of New England and the Middle Atlantic states, where the plentiful water power enabled millowners to run machinery inexpensively.

The emergence of the factory system created a new problem—a human one. There was a shortage of workers to operate the machines. If a man was not a small farmer, he practiced a trade either as a skilled craftsman or a journeyman. Such men would not accept employment in a factory. Millowners, the new breed of merchant capitalist, looked for a new labor supply.

They chose one with incredible callousness.

Late in the eighteenth century, as the first textile mills were being built, one of the earliest factories employed nine children less than twelve years old. A decade later that same factory had more than 100 children whose ages ranged between four and ten working in it.

The shocking practice of putting young boys and girls in factories was not universally frowned upon. The nation's first Secretary of the Treasury, Alexander Hamilton, strongly supported child labor. He said:

"It is worthy of particular remark that in general . . . children are rendered useful . . . by manufacturing establishments than they otherwise would be . . ."

At a time when schooling was costly and attainable only by the wealthy, working-class children received no education. In Pennsylvania, for example, 250,000 children out of 400,000 had no education at all. These illiterate children provided a vast labor reservoir; they could be taught the simple jobs of tending looms and machines in mills and factories.

Thus, by 1820, over half the factory workers in the United States were nine- and ten-year-olds, toiling an average of thirteen hours a day. For this work, the boys and girls received salaries ranging between 33 cents and 67 cents per *week*. Small wonder that manufacturers eagerly sought this cheap labor. Almost every edition of daily newspapers in New England and other industrial areas carried advertisements reading:

children provided cheap labor in early factories

HELP WANTED: A family of five to eight children capable of working in a cotton mill.

Unfortunately, working-class parents, trying to eke out a living, willingly sent their children to work at an early age; the few pennies they earned helped buy bread. Poverty throttled sentiment; the struggle for existence was a desperate one. Childhood ended quickly and joylessly in those days.

Women were another source of low-paid labor. Agents of factory operators combed the countryside to recruit girls from farms and villages to work in mills. An agent received a fee for each young woman he signed up. The girls contracted to work for stipulated periods; a year was usually the minimal length of time. In a sense, this made them indentured workers except that the employer was obliged to pay wages.

Slick-talking agents lured thousands of young women and teen-age girls from rural areas with enticing descriptions of the glamorous life that awaited female factory workers. The girls were promised excitement, fine clothes, high wages and plenty of time off.

The unsophisticated country lasses soon learned that they had been duped. Instead of fun and leisure they found drudgery and virtual slavery. The drab mill towns were mean and ugly; the air was tainted by foul smoke belching from factory chimneys.

"Oh, dear God, I wish to be dead . . . I am enslaved in this dreadful place . . . There is no sweetness, no beauty, no joy . . . only clacking looms, whirring wheels and clattering machinery . . . Never a glimpse of blue sky, no dancing sunbeams, no sweet-smelling new mown hay . . . this factory is an earthly hell . . ." a nineteen-year-old girl wrote to a friend back home.

The unhappy letter writer was not exaggerating her plight. Women workers in the mills led lives of wearisome toil. From 5 A.M. until 7:30 P.M., six days a week, the girls carded wool, tended looms, pressed, folded and packed finished cloth. At noon they had a quarter of an hour lunch break, barely time enough to gulp down the watery soup and chunk of stale bread provided by the management.

For their daily fourteen-hour stint the women were paid wages that averaged between $2 and $2.50 per week. Half of this sum went back to the company as rent for a cot in the factory-owned boarding-house dormitory—which usually adjoined the factory—where the workers had to live. The food they were given was "slops . . . such as we would not feed hogs on the farm . . .," a worker noted. Legally bound by a year's contract, the millhands had to endure the abominable conditions imposed by the company.

Sunday, their only day off, the girls had to spend in stern Puritan fashion. The Sabbath was marked by "prayer, meditation and spiritual purification." Factory owners saw no contradiction between the treatment accorded their workers and insistence on rigid observation of the Lord's Day.

"Some have accused us of harshness to our employees. Hard work is good for the soul and prayer a bulwark against Satan. We do not intend to let the Evil One capture the innocent girls in our charge . . . Our credo is "Work and Prayer," a millowner piously declared. "He might have added 'profit' to his motto," a journalist remarked.

With the entry of women and children into the labor market and the steadily increasing number of factories, the changing industrial pattern was causing grave distress among skilled craftsmen and mechanics. As more factories produced ever-growing volumes of once exclusively handmade products, the nation's artisans suffered a severe economic pinch. They could not compete in price with the factories, nor could they match in quantity the manufactured goods that flooded out to an eager public.

"No one cares about good work any more," a disgruntled Philadelphia master shoemaker complained. "It no longer matters whether an article is well-made; the only concern nowadays is that it must be low-priced."

As though the impact of factory-made products was not crushing enough, master craftsmen, along with other Americans, received still another blow, even more crippling. A financial and economic depression swept the United States in 1819, bringing with it mass unemployment and hunger. Businesses fell into bankruptcy by the hundreds; factories closed; small shops and stores went dark.

Textile mills and other factories in the Northeast which survived the depression's initial shock, kept going by cutting wages and lengthening working hours. Any employee who complained was promptly fired; there were scores waiting for jobs outside the factory gate. Master craftsmen who once had received the highest wages were now glad to get work for $2 a week.

The depression hung over the land until 1822, and in those three years most of the trade unions formed since 1800 were wiped out. But as business gradually recovered and employment rose, the workers returned to unionism with new zeal.

Like the tremors of an earthquake, a wave of strikes in almost every trade rocked city after city. Masons, carpenters, tailors, seamen, shoemakers, stonecutters, upholsterers, cabinetmakers—workers of all kinds—fought to win back the wage scales and working conditions they had attained before the bleak days of 1819–1822.

Everywhere workers raised the cry for more pay and shorter hours. Some struggles they won; some they lost. A lesson was learned from the defeats. The small craft unions did not have enough strength or money to hold out against an employer who was willing to endure a long strike.

"Let them tramp the streets; I'll outlast them. I can afford to close shop. But sooner or later, they'll come crawling back," a Massachusetts factory owner said. "They can't feed their kids on slogans!"

It became increasingly clear to unionists that what happened to one union affected all. This was brought home in 1827 when the carpenters of Philadelphia launched a city-wide strike for the 10-hour working day. The carpenters lost the long and bitter fight that ensued. Since no other union had come to aid the carpenters, the chances grew slimmer for any to achieve a 10-hour day.

"Had we fought together, every worker would have benefited by the victory," a union leader said. "In unity there is strength!"

The Philadelphia unions decided to prove this. Before the end of 1827, they formed a central union council, called the Mechanics Union of Trade Associations. It was the first city-wide labor organization in the world. By 1836, some thirteen cities in the United States had similar groups.

The Philadelphia workers paved the way for political as well as economic action by forming the Workingmen's Party—the world's first labor party. The idea caught on and spread. From 1828 to 1834, Workingmen's Parties appeared on the ballot in sixty-one cities and towns. Rich businessmen listened in dismay as labor chanted its demands—free and equal public education, the restriction of child labor, the universal 10-hour day, abolition of imprisonment for debt and other reforms.

No matter what else the workers wanted, they first sought free education for their children. "There can be no liberty without knowledge . . . no democracy without education," a unionist wrote in a labor paper.

Almost every leaflet, pamphlet or circular published by the Workingmen's Party called for an end to what was termed a "vicious relic of feudal tyranny"—imprisonment for debt. According to a report made in 1834, over 75,000 people were jailed annually as debtors. Of these, about 50 per cent owed less than $20, some as little as $1. No matter how small the sum, a creditor could have a man thrown into prison until the debt was paid.

Once a man was in a jail cell, he had no way of earning the money to pay off his obligation. As a result, the debtors' prisons were always crowded; some inmates had been incarcerated for years. The conditions in these places were unspeakable.

"The prison reeked of unwashed humanity . . . It crawled with vermin . . . and diseases flourished within the dank walls. The poor wretches trapped there had lost all hope and courage . . . they stared dully at the squalor and misery which surrounded them. This was indeed the abyss of despair . . ." a newspaper reporter wrote after a visit to a debtors' prison.

Ironically, the authorities provided no food for imprisoned debtors; family and friends brought rations and those miserable souls who had no one, relied on the bones and scraps left by their fellow-inmates. Small wonder that so many sickened and died. However, criminals of the worst sort were fed by the state.

"A man who had committed a murder was better off than one imprisoned for debt . . . how absurd and revolting is the cruel and oppressive law which makes poverty a crime and a poor man worse than a felon . . ." a historian observed.

The Workingmen's Party entered slates in several cities after 1829 and in Philadelphia elected twenty of its fifty-four candidates. The Party also did well in New York, where Ebenezer Ford, president of the carpenters' union, was elected to the state assembly. Elsewhere, throughout the country, the workers' nominees captured local offices.

Bosses warned that any worker who voted for the Workingmen's Party would be fired. In those days the secret ballot was not yet in use. A voter told the recording clerk his choice of candidates. Many workers defied their employers and were discharged for voting for the Workingmen's Party, when spies reported them to the boss.

Newspapers labeled the Workingmen's Party "radical," "anti-religious," "the great unwashed rabble," "the dirty shirts," "the rag tag and bobtail" and stronger derogatory terms. Nor did the labor party's foes limit their campaign against it to words. Workingmen's Party meetings were packed with hoodlums, thugs and "goons" hired by local politicians. The rowdies heckled speakers and provoked fights. Many workers' rallies ended in bloody brawls.

Such attacks weakened the Workingmen's Party. Many members were scared off by violence, the fear of job loss or other reprisals. But the greatest flaw in the movement was the internal defect of the Party's structure. The leaders had little or no political experience and were often uncertain about policies.

The membership consisted mainly of skilled craftsmen; but many workers in the United States were either common laborers or factory hands and did not belong to the Party. In fact, since most factory workers were women, who did not have the right to vote, or children, not old enough to cast a ballot, Party leaders made no effort to include them in their program.

Divergent views on how to best help the working class split the Party's unity. Some believed workers should establish their own communities; others felt that the evils of the time could be eliminated only by federal grants of free land to the poor, thus making America an agrarian, not an industrial, nation.

Perhaps the most important reason the Workingmen's Party finally disappeared from the scene was Andrew Jackson's re-election to the Presidency in 1832. "Old Hickory" had shown himself to be the workers' friend. He was a "son of the soil," a fighter for the people against the rich. The workers trusted "Andy" and showed it by sending him back to the White House for a second term.

With Jackson as Chief Executive, many workers felt there was no longer a need for keeping alive their own party. The President had spoken out strongly in the people's behalf, saying:

"When the laws undertake to make the rich richer and the potent more powerful, the humble members of society, the farmers, mechanics and laborers, who have neither the time nor the means of securing like favors for themselves, have a right to complain of the injustice of their government . . ."

By 1834, the Workingmen's Party ceased to exist. But in six short years it had forced the passage of many social and economic reforms. Imprisonment for debt was abolished; public school systems were established. In 1834, Pennsylvania led the way, setting up the nation's first tax-supported free schools.

Many benefits enjoyed today by those who work for a living stem from reforms demanded by workers in 1828. Conditions now taken for granted as the basic rights of our citizens were won long ago by men and women who possessed the courage and foresight to wage the struggle for better lives for themselves, their children and future generations.

This is a frequently forgotten heritage from America's past. This was the great American dream: that every man might be able to earn his living in decency and dignity.

On July 4, 1828, Charles Carroll, the last living signer of the Declaration of Independence, participated in an unusual ceremony. He officiated at the track laying of the Baltimore and Ohio Railroad, the nation's first railway.

As the spike was driven, the clanging sledge hammer resounded across the land. The advent of the railroad marked a complete break with the past. Within a few years rail networks spread like tentacles across mountains and rivers, prairies and grasslands, carrying people and products in numbers and quantities never before believed possible. Centers of commerce and industry grew up wherever the railroads went.

In the three decades between 1830 and 1860 the country developed at an incredible pace. There were but 17 miles of track in 1830 and the value of manufactured goods was $300,-000,000. By 1860, over 30,000 miles of railroad track formed a communication skein across the eastern half of the nation and the value of manufactured goods had risen to more than $2,000,-000,000. Those thirty years saw the most remarkable growth ever achieved in any country. The United States matured into a lusty, dynamic industrial giant, pulsating with energy and vitality.

The 1840's witnessed a tremendous surge westward beyond the Appalachian Mountains. What had once been pioneer land, holding only a few thousand settlers, now teemed with new cities, towns, villages, farms and factories. Into the region swarmed more than 8,000,000 inhabitants. The victorious war with Mexico (1846–1848) added vast new territories to the United States; the Stars and Stripes was planted in California, Texas, New Mexico and Arizona.

The country sprawled from "sea to shining sea." There was room to breathe, move and expand. In 1849, the discovery of gold in California brought thousands of eager fortune seekers there; gold and silver strikes in Nevada and Montana a few years later attracted more treasure hunters. Many made the long trek. Some failed and crept back East; a few struck it rich; some stayed to settle the fertile western lands.

Prior to 1840, immigration to the United States from Europe had been relatively limited. Most Europeans who ventured to the New World were farmers. After 1840, immigrants came in droves, and they were a new breed.

From Germany came working-class revolutionaries, fresh from the barricades where they had fought for "Republicanism." When their democratic revolution failed in 1848, these high-minded rebels fled by the thousands to refuge in America. Among them were skilled workers such as mechanics, cabinet-makers, furniture polishers, carpenters and watchmakers. They were hard-working, socially-conscious men and women, an asset to the growing nation. That same fateful year, 1848, a potato famine in Ireland caused a mass exodus to America from the starvation and misery in that blighted land.

If the newcomers to America's shores expected warm-hearted acceptance, they were sorely disappointed. Instead of a welcome they found hostility, suspicion and violence. The Roman Catholic Irish were made the special targets of bigotry and intolerance. Self-styled "patriots" formed anti-Catholic organizations and hapless Irishmen suffered at their hands.

This foreign influx crowded cities such as New York, Boston and Philadelphia; housing was inadequate and the immigrants were forced to live in dreadful, disease-ridden slums. The filth and squalor of these horrible places "made the mind reel."

An official report drawn up by the New York City Metropolitan Police Department in 1850 estimated that more than 5,000 persons were living in cellars. During heavy rainstorms, these dank holes often were flooded by backwash from overflowing gutters and people actually drowned in bed. Health investigators found families huddled in rooms "without air, without light, filled with damp vapour from mildewed walls, crawling with lice and rats . . . the most repulsive holes ever occupied by human beings. . ."

Still, immigrants from Europe streamed to America's shores. Some did not linger on the Atlantic seaboard but pushed out to the newer cities in the Midwest. Soon, nearly half the population of cities, such as Chicago and St. Louis, were foreign-born. By 1860, about 300,000 of New York's 800,000 residents were immigrants.

The foreigners provided cheap labor; the Irish filled railroad building work gangs, while Germans went into the factories which were coming up on every side. The "greenhorns" (a slang term for immigrants) were hired at lower wages than Americans and bigots used this to fan smoldering animosity between native-born and foreign-born.

Americans looked upon "greenhorns" as a "pestilence" dragging down living standards and working conditions. An anti-foreign pamphlet charged that immigrants were "subhuman beings . . . feeding upon the coarsest food . . . wearing the worst clothes . . . and having the habits of swine . . . not fit associates for American laborers and mechanics nor any decent members of society . . ."

51

immigrants landing at Castle Garden, 1855

The United States was passing through its time of "growing pains," an awkward transitional period of adolescence when nothing seemed constant or certain. In those crucial thirty years (1830–1860), the Industrial Revolution burst upon America. Many factors contributed to the rapid rate of industrial growth, but the railroads, which opened ever widening markets, played the largest role.

Virtually no corner of the country (except the Far West and areas of the South) was not within reach of a railroad. In 1860, the first transcontinental rail lines were being laid. Within a few years, the United States was girdled by several cross-country railroads.

This was the era when "Big Industry" made its bow. The small cotton mills of New England blossomed into huge textile plants. For instance, in 1840, about 2,300,000 spindles were operating. Twenty years later, more than 5,000,000 spindles spun cloth in Northern mills.

Railroad construction increased the demand for iron and scores of new foundries belched smoke from their stacks. But the old methods of producing iron were no longer adequate; blast furnaces for converting iron into steel came into existence. Great numbers of unskilled workers were required by the steel plants. More iron ore had to be dug. The 180,000 tons of iron ore produced in 1830 soared to 980,000 tons within thirty years.

The huge furnaces had to be fired by coal. Soon, coalfields were employing great numbers of workers in West Virginia and Pennsylvania. Coal mining was a dirty, dangerous occupation and Americans shunned the work; but immigrants, glad for a chance at any job, flocked to dig the coal out of the reluctant earth, working like moles in the dark shafts that honeycombed the fields.

More and more American craftsmen, unable to maintain their own small shops, went to work in factories. A half million of them took up such employment from 1840–1860. The day of small shops and hand craftsmanship was almost at an end.

As industrialization increased, the fertile minds and imaginations of American inventors turned to developing labor-saving devices. Year by year, Yankee ingenuity made production more mechanized. In that same thirty-year span (1830–1860) the number of patents granted to American inventors soared amazingly. The United States government issued 544 patents in 1830; twenty years later the number rose to 933 and by 1860 had jumped to 4,778. There were more machine patents granted in the United States during those years than in England and France combined.

The Machine Age had dawned.

The working forces in factories swelled ever larger and as a result, the chasm between employer and employees increased. This impersonal relationship was succinctly stated by one New England millowner:

"So long as my hired hands do my work for what I choose to pay them, I keep them, getting out of them all I can. What they do or how they are outside my walls I don't know nor do I consider it my business to know. They must look out for themselves as I do for myself. When my machines get old and useless I reject them and get new ones and these people are part of my machinery . . ."

This was blunt language, but it represented the prevailing attitude of capital toward labor when America rushed full tilt into the industrial era.

American workers hated the Machine Age.

They detested the mines, mills, plants and factories that scarred the countryside, fouled streams and rivers, and poisoned the air with clouds of soft coal smoke. They loathed the din and grime. To them, the factory whistle was "a screeching banshee." They saw the growth of industry as "slow death," not progress.

A labor editor wrote:

"On every side we see scabrous factories rising in fields where once wild flowers grew . . . We are no longer masters of our fate, but slaves to insensate machines . . ."

The workers felt degraded and humiliated by the machines, driven to a lower social level, a way of life destroyed, old standards swept away. This was a time that shattered a man, robbing him of his former pride as a craftsman. The workers fought against the implacable enemy. Strikes erupted in a score of cities, several led by the girls of the textile mills.

The bosses used many weapons to crush these labor revolts. Blacklists circulated from millowner to millowner and unionists found themselves without jobs or the hope of getting one. Brutal violence was unleashed against strikers; men were beaten, even murdered, for leading a walkout.

The struggle between capital and labor became war, merciless and unrelenting, with no holds barred. The capitalists refused to yield an inch, no matter how just the workers' demands might be. This was the way of the new order. Small wonder that oppressed workers sought frantically for an escape and often grasped at unrealistic schemes.

Reformers developed visionary ideas; some had merit, others were vague dreams based on wild-eyed premises. George Henry Evans, editor of the *New York Working Man's Advocate*, urged the "masses of wage slaves" to escape the evils of industrialization by going West and becoming farmers. "The poor must work in the factories or starve . . . unless they can cultivate the land," he said.

The prospects of owning land in the wide West, of breathing clean air and living independently on a farm, appealed to many. But moving West was not so simple for the average worker. After 1820, Western public land was sold by the government in 160-acre parcels at $1.25 an acre. To buy a farm meant an investment of at least $200 for land; in an era when a factory worker's salary ranged from $2.50 to $5.80 per week, $200 represented a huge sum.

But there was more to settling out West than simply buying a tract. Travel was expensive; a man had to have a wagon, oxen, food and equipment. Once at his destination, he needed farming tools, seed and the material to build a cabin. It was estimated that the lowest stake needed to start a farm was $600. More likely it would require about $1,000 to cover expenses and emergencies.

Between 1840 and 1860, thousands of Eastern workers somehow scrimped to save the necessary funds and took up life anew on the vast frontier; but for most, a farm remained only a vision. Poverty proved an unsurmountable barrier.

Evans proposed to overcome this handicap by means of a Federal free land program; the U.S. government should give to any applicant a 106-acre plot out West if the recipient agreed to cultivate the soil for a specified time.

Many workers rallied around Evans; the free land movement appealed to them. It offered an escape to trapped and down-trodden factory workers. Evans predicted his plan would also help improve the lot of workers who did not take a land grant but preferred to stay in the city. If enough workingmen went West, he reasoned, a labor shortage would be created in the factories. Those who remained could then wrest better conditions from the bosses by threatening to leave and go West.

"Without a ready supply of workers to exploit, the capitalists no longer will have free rein; at long last the voices of those who toil shall be heard and their rightful demands met," the editor prophesied.

The free land crusade which began in 1840 was to last twenty years. In 1860, Abraham Lincoln, Presidential candidate of the newly formed Republican Party, included free land as a plank in his election platform. Workers, farmers, and reformers flocked to Lincoln's support, raising the campaign slogan: "Vote For Abe and Vote Yourself A Farm!"

With Lincoln in the White House, Evans' long fight was won. In 1862, as the Civil War raged, Congress passed the Homestead Act which provided for the free distribution of 106-acre parcels to all applicants willing to farm the land.

Hordes of workers took advantage of the Homestead Act; but the great westward migration did not put an end to industrial abuses. Not everyone was suited for farming and many once-hopeful escapees went back East after a few discouraging years trying to scratch a living from the soil.

They returned to mine, mill, plant and factory where

58

low wages and bad working conditions still prevailed and the bosses ruled as despotically as ever. The American workingman seemed unable to better his lot. The trade unions still functioning were weak and poorly organized. Several labor leaders of the time blamed the lack of strong unions on the desire of the American worker for self-employment and independence.

"Instead of building his unions, he chases rainbows and dreams of getting away from it all . . . of being a farmer . . . The Free Land Reform has harmed the average worker more than it has helped him . . ." a labor editor wrote.

Charles Beard, the noted historian, pointed out why the American trade unions of the 1850's had not reached the militant level of those in Europe:

"Energies which in the normal course of affairs would have been devoted to building up trade unions and framing schemes for social revolution were diverted to agitation in favor of a free farm for every workingman whether he wanted it or not . . ."

During the two decades of the free land crusade, workers pushed other plans aimed at freeing them from "wage slavery." They settled in communities known as "phalanxes" where rich and poor, craftsmen, common laborers and intellectuals lived together in an atmosphere of "communal brotherhood." Each of these high-minded experiments failed although one "phalanx" managed to last more than thirteen years.

Horace Greeley, editor of the *New York Tribune*, was an enthusiastic advocate of "phalanxes" and similar utopian innovations. He particularly spoke out in favor of what was known as a "producing cooperative." Under this plan, workers of diverse skills would settle in a community and run their own shops to produce all sorts of products. The profits realized from selling the cooperative-made goods on the open market would then be shared by the entire community.

Time, toil, sweat and tears were spent to create producing cooperatives. Workers in Cincinnati, Boston, Philadelphia, Pittsburgh, New York, Wheeling and Providence, tried desperately to keep their cooperatives alive. Iron molders, glass blowers, seamstresses, hatters, tailors, carpenters and mechanics banded together and struggled valiantly, but the odds against success were too great. The producing cooperatives were doomed at their inception.

Because they were artisans, not businessmen, the workers made many mistakes in running the cooperatives. Their major error was in attempting to operate without sufficient capital. As one cooperative after another failed, a leader of the movement said, "We have swallowed a bitter draught; due to the lack of funds, we must shut down . . . We were foolish to believe faith could take the place of cold cash . . ."

There was no way for the cooperatives to raise the necessary capital. No bank would back them. Even the most reckless speculators refused to risk investment in such unorthodox ventures. The only financial support came from workers who could not afford to give much money.

Thus, the producing cooperatives into which men had poured strength, hope and prayers, withered and died. The dream lived on in men's hearts and minds but could not survive the reality of a society which had no sympathy for idealists and dreamers. It was a society where money ruled.

"Mammon is God!" a New England preacher thundered from his pulpit. "There has risen among us a breed of men who worship the Golden Calf and not the Golden Rule! To them, the dollar sign has replaced the Cross!"

Despite such denunciations, the capitalists did not alter their behavior. They forced workers to accept the lowest pay for the longest hours of work. Factory conditions, which had been bad enough before, became intolerable.

"We must work faster, faster and ever faster . . . until it has become unbearable . . . They drive us without pity . . . Surely the lot of the enslaved blacks can be no worse than ours—and we are called freemen! What a cruel jest!" a Massachusetts textile worker wrote.

During the 1840's and 1850's, American workers refused to accept an inevitable fate and would not concede that the Industrial Revolution was permanent. The workers wanted to keep the old order and tried by every means to escape the realities of the Industrial Revolution. However, neither free land, cooperatives, phalanxes nor visionary communities could solve the problems of the working class.

At last, they reluctantly confronted the real issues. After having followed reformers for almost two decades and wasted energy in vague causes, American workers abandoned their efforts to build a society based on social justice and humanitarianism. To end abuses in the factories, the workers had to fight the capitalists, and their best weapon in that struggle was the trade unions.

Even while most workers were engaged in reform movements, some had kept the unions alive. These men also supported the reformists, backed the free land fight, entered into producing cooperatives and yearned for a society where one could work in a "spirit of humanity," a society without poverty and want, where people could live in dignity and comfort. However, unlike the reformers, the union-conscious workers were not concerned solely with a vague, idyllic social system. They also tackled the more immediate problems of wages and hours.

"We can see sweet visions far out beyond the horizon; perhaps the dreams will come true for our children, or our children's children; but we must keep alive to sire future generations . . . what we gain today will help build tomorrow . . ." declared a union leader.

As the 1850's drew to a close, more and more workers turned from reformism to unionism. Since there seemed to be no escape from industrialization, and the old days were forever vanished, the workers braced for battle to win a betterment of working conditions, an end to brutal speedup, higher wages, the 10-hour day.

The revived unions limited membership to skilled mechanics and craftsmen. It was felt that not only machines but also the semi-skilled and unskilled workers who operated them, were undermining the craftsmen; hence membership in craft unions was restricted to skilled men.

Most unions admitted only native-born Americans. Some American mechanics feared the rising tide of immigration. They saw their hard-earned working and living standards being swept away by "greenhorns" who "willingly accepted work at any pay and under any circumstances . . ." Anti-foreign labor leaders charged that the immigrants were "imported scabs," hired as strikebreakers.

Nothing could have been farther from the truth. Most of the skilled foreign workers had been socialists and ardent trade unionists in their own country. German craftsmen who had shed blood fighting for democracy in 1848 would have rushed to join a trade union had they not been excluded by prejudiced Americans.

The main foes of the immigrants were fanatical nationalists. These extremists had formed a political party, the Native Americans, commonly called the "Know-Nothings." The primary purpose of this group was to end further immigration into the United States. In some cities, Know-Nothings organized riots against foreigners and loosed a reign of terror upon them. They masked this unjust action by claiming to "protect the American worker against foreign interlopers . . ."

Actually, they were serving the capitalists who exploited them. The employers did everything possible to encourage immigration. Skilled foreign mechanics and artisans gave the bosses an excellent hold over American workers. So long as the native-born pitted themselves against foreigners, trade unions worked at a handicap, hamstrung by the split in the working class. If Americans demanded higher wages, the employers could threaten to hire foreigners; should the greenhorns express discontent, the bosses warned that they would be fired and replaced by Americans. Because of bigotry and intolerance, the capitalists could have free rein.

A discerning millowner pithily summed up the predicament of the unions. "We are delighted to heap coals on the feud between Americans and immigrants . . . While they fight each other, the workers cannot fight us effectively . . ."

Many trade union leaders recognized their plight. A leading labor editor wrote an impassioned editorial in which he said:

"American Mechanics! Brothers, recollect that you must unite as mechanics and as mechanics only. The feeling of animosity which exists against foreign mechanics was initiated by employers to distract your attention from the real struggle . . . the fight to better the lot of all workers! Americans! Do not allow yourselves to be deluded by small-minded men who speak out of hatred, bias and stupidity. You must unite!"

Unfortunately the seeds of intolerance had been too deeply implanted. Only a few craft unions understood the situation and opened their rosters to foreigners.

Nor were immigrants the only victims of working-class intolerance. In shops which hired women, unions refused to enroll female workers. Although women often did the same tasks as men, they were paid much less. Some far-sighted unionists raised the slogan, "Equal pay for equal work!" But as long as craft unions barred women workers, there remained the double wage standard.

Again, unions had provided employers with a weapon. If male workers grew too militant, the boss throttled their demands by threatening to hire women in their place. The great struggle for industrial democracy had to be waged within the unions as well as against the bosses. It was destined to be a long and arduous fight. Intolerance and bigotry were not to be easily erased.

800 women shoemakers on strike in Lynn, Massachusetts, 1860

Although the resurgent craft unions had many short-comings, they gained strength. Local unions, which formerly had suffered from slipshod management, now were run efficiently. Dues collection was strictly enforced. A special fund was earmarked for strike benefits. All locals held regular membership meetings.

Workers no longer were satisfied to win concessions in a single shop. Instead, they sought city-wide agreements on wages, hours and working conditions for all employees in the same trade or industry.

But markets were not limited to specific areas. Business now was conducted on a national scale. In each city, wages and hours varied, depending on the state of the local unions. It soon became clear to unionists that wage scales had to be standardized on a national basis.

Individual local unions could not cope with rapidly spreading industry. Obviously, if business was conducted nationally, labor unions must also reach beyond the local scene and each craft had to form nationwide unions for the protection of all workers everywhere in the United States.

In 1852 journeymen printers from six states met at New York City for the purpose of building an "extensive organization embracing the entire country." At this gathering was born the National Typographical Union (N.T.U.), the first permanent national union. From time to time, since 1834, attempts had been made to found national labor organizations. But until the N.T.U., all efforts had failed.

The printers called upon fellow-workers to "close ranks and unite to bring about the betterment of all." The N.T.U. proposed a standard wage throughout the printing industry; members were to be issued travel certificates so that a man could work in any union shop under the same conditions he had enjoyed at his former job.

A strike fund upon which every branch of the national union might call was to be created. In order that "scabs" and "rats" who had been expelled as strikebreakers in one town might not join the union in another, the national office intended to publish a list naming these undesirables and circulate it among all locals of the N.T.U. The precedent set by the printers soon was followed by hat finishers, stone cutters, cigar makers, iron molders and others. At least ten national unions were organized between 1850 and 1860.

Building a national union was slow, tedious work that called for dedicated and persevering men. There were many such in the labor movement, but the most outstanding was William Sylvis of the Iron Molders Union. Born in 1828 at Armagh, Pensylvania, Sylvis was the son of a wagonmaker. Apprenticed as an iron molder at the age of ten, he worked and sweated countless hours in an iron foundry.

A full-fledged journeyman before he was twenty, Sylvis joined the Philadelphia local of the Iron Molders Union and before long became its recording secretary. His local was the strongest of the union's seventeen branches scattered around the country. The militant Philadelphia iron molders had won good working conditions for themselves, although members of locals in other cities had not fared so well.

A financial panic swept the United States in 1857 and along with the rest of the nation, the iron molders suffered heavily during the year-long depression that followed. Wages in the industry were slashed and many jobs eliminated as iron works in different part of the country either merged or consolidated. Where the locals were weakest, employers forced speed up, extra hours and other abuses on their workers.

By 1859, the national economy began to recover. As business started booming once more, Sylvis decided that the time was at hand to press for the formation of a national iron molders union. He wrote other locals suggesting that a convention of molders be held in Philadelphia to discuss the formation of such a union. His idea met with an enthusiastic response.

On July 5, 1859, thirty-five delegates from twelve locals met at Philadelphia and formed the National Iron Molders Union. "Single-handed we can accomplish nothing," Sylvis told the convention. "United there is no power of wrong we cannot openly defy . . ."

The union flourished despite the many strikes it had to lead against stubborn employers who would not yield to basic demands without a fight. But the outbreak of the Civil War in 1861 stunted the union's growth and by 1863, when Sylvis became its president, the once-mighty organization had all but withered away.

The war's impact had proved almost too much; hundreds of members were off in the army; the national treasury was almost depleted; a number of locals had collapsed and Sylvis ruled over a dying body. He was determined to revive the union in the only way he knew, which was "to go out among the workers and speak to them man to man . . . and together find the means for rebuilding our union . . ."

Sylvis borrowed $100 from the Philadelphia local and embarked on what he called a "tour of experiment." With no other funds he traveled almost 10,000 miles in a year, visiting every section of the United States and even going into Canada.

"Wherever there was an iron foundry, I made an appearance. . . ." he said.

The union missionary hitched rides from town to town, ate when he could and slept in barns or open fields. An iron molder wrote of Sylvis:

"He wore his clothes until they became quite threadbare and he could wear them no longer . . . the shawl he wore to the day of his death was filled with holes burned there by the splashing of molten iron from the ladles of molders in strange cities whom he was beseeching to organize . . ."

The workers listened to Sylvis. They respected this crusader who had thrown himself into the battle with such fervor. The molders heeded his words and regrouped their shattered ranks.

By the end of the year, Sylvis had accomplished a miracle of organization. He had formed eighteen new locals, revived sixteen dead locals and placed twelve old ones on a solid footing. All this was achieved by one man at great personal sacrifice; that year ruined Sylvis' health and brought on the tuberculosis which would take his life in 1869.

"I love this union cause," Sylvis once said. "I am willing to devote to it all that I am, or have, or hope for in the world."

By 1865, when the Civil War ended, many fresh problems piled upon the labor movement. New factories had risen to supply Northern armies with guns, clothing, shoes and a thousand other items. Everywhere furnaces roared, hammers clanged and chimneys poured out smoke.

Industry had made a tremendous upsurge during the war years. With the conflict over, Northern manufacturing interests emerged triumphant. They controlled the country. Since high tariffs now barred foreign-made goods, Yankee industrialists no longer feared European competition. They had been given a mandate to fix prices, amass profits and crush the labor movement.

The industrialists also had been handed a powerful cudgel to use against the unions. In 1864, Congress had passed a contract labor law. This legislation, enacted to ensure sufficient manpower for the industries which supplied the Yankee armies, allowed manufacturers in the United States to import European workingmen.

The employer paid the immigrant's passage and the foreigner contracted to work for his American boss over a given period at a stipulated wage, one that was much lower than an American worker's. Each week some of the fare was deducted. The prevailing pay for immigrant contract labor was so low and the fare deductions so small that an employer was sure of getting at least a year's work out of his contract employee.

In addition to foreign workers, the labor market was glutted by a flood of newly freed Negro slaves. Millions of them poured out of the South, glad to take any job at any wage. The skilled craftsmen hated both Negroes and immigrants and looked upon them as the foes of a decent American standard of living. Only a few labor leaders understood that the manufacturing overlords and powerful industrialists were the real enemies of the American working class.

A labor paper, the *Boston Evening Voice*, stated in an editorial:

"Why does capital roll in luxury and wealth while labor is left to eke out a miserable existence in poverty and want? The reason is crystal clear . . . the minions of capital have learned well the dictum, 'Divide and Conquer!' Have they not succeeded in turning one workingman against the other? The white man against the black; the native-born against the foreigner . . . Is the time not at hand when labor must close ranks and bring to bear all its might against the common foe?"

The Growing Time

1865–1900

After the Civil War the South was torn and bleeding.
Her plantations lay in blackened ruins; the slave system, upon which her economy was based, had been ended.
Only diehard Confederates still dreamed that one day the old
ways would be restored.

The Southern "aristocracy" had been overthrown and
"King Cotton" deposed. Now steel, meat, coal and oil sat on
the throne of industry. At night, the skies over Pittsburgh
glowed red with the reflections of blast furnace fires. The
stench of Chicago's stockyards choked that city. The first oil
derricks rose near Titusville, Pennsylvania, to pump up the
"black gold" that flowed beneath the earth. Trains rattled daily
over wide plains where only yesterday Indians had hunted buffalo. All America throbbed and pulsated to the rhythms of
pounding, clanging machinery.

American industry created its own titans, such men as
E. H. Harriman and Jay Gould, who controlled a railroad em-
pire; Andrew Carnegie, the Steel King; John D. Rockefeller,
the Oil Czar. There were many others—financiers, bankers, the
giants and monarchs of industry.

Less than a year after the Civil War had ended, a labor
paper warned:

"Capital is centralizing, organizing and becoming more
powerful every day. The late war and what has grown out of
the war, made Capital stronger. It has made millions at

the expense of the labor of this country, and the capital thus concentrated is to be used in a greater or lesser degree to defeat the objects sought by the workingmen . . ."

Nineteenth-century American industrialists regarded labor as a commodity, to be bought, sold or discarded at will. As management became stronger, pressure against the workers increased to such an extent that unions had difficulty holding the ground they had already gained. In this situation they could hardly raise demands for other benefits such as the 8-hour day. The fight for the 10-hour day had been won back in the 1850's. Now a movement to make an 8-hour work day the standard had sprung up, and many "Eight Hour Leagues" were formed.

Aware that action had to be taken on a major scale, labor leaders looked for a means to break industry's throttling grip. A union journal offered one solution to labor's dilemma:

"What must we workers do to combat the stranglehold of capital? We must unite ourselves in a union of unions . . . and establish a national labor federation . . . Thus, we will present a solid front to our enemies and cement the unity among the working class throughout all the states . . ."

The suggestion was not a new one. The idea of such a federation had been raised before and several futile efforts made to launch one. Now the time seemed ripe to try again. Accordingly, a group of trade union leaders sent out a call for a national labor convention. The response was gratifying. Seventy-seven delegates from fifty local unions, thirteen city trade councils, two national unions and five eight-hour leagues gathered in Baltimore on August 20, 1866.

The hall in which they met was decorated with crossed American flags, trade union banners and bunting. Over the podium hung a huge placard upon which was lettered: "Wel-

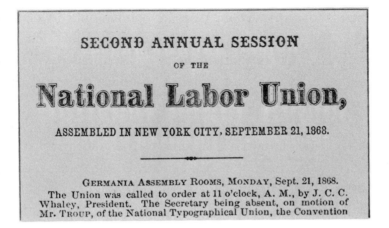

SECOND ANNUAL SESSION

OF THE

National Labor Union,

ASSEMBLED IN NEW YORK CITY, SEPTEMBER 21, 1868.

GERMANIA ASSEMBLY ROOMS, MONDAY, Sept. 21, 1868.
The Union was called to order at 11 o'clock, A. M., by J. C. C.
Whaley, President. The Secretary being absent, on motion of
Mr. TROUP, of the National Typographical Union, the Convention

come to the Sons of Toil from North, South, East and West!"
It was a red letter day for the labor movement; the first time in
American history that workers from every section of the country
actually had come together to form a countrywide "union of
unions." This was accomplished by the convention, which
launched the National Labor Union (N.L.U.).

High on the agenda of the newborn federation was the
8-hour day issue. The delegates passed a resolution which
stated:

> ". . . the first and great necessity of the present to free the
> laborers of this country from capitalistic slavery is the pass-
> ing of a law by which eight hours shall be the normal
> working day in all states of the American Union . . ."

From the outset, the N.L.U. showed itself to be more re-
formist than radical. The 8-hour day was to be won by "passing
a law" and not through direct action, such as work stoppages
and strikes.

The convention made another important decision—the
N.L.U. intended to enter the field of politics by forming a

national labor party. As one delegate pointed out: "A new party of the people must be in the minority when it first comes into being. Well, what of that? Time and perseverance will give us victory; and if we are not willing to sacrifice time and employ perseverance, we are not deserving of victory . . ."

William Sylvis, unable to attend the convention because of illness, made known his support of the labor party. He also backed the stand adopted by the N.L.U. on other vital labor questions. The federation came out for organizing unskilled workers, backed land reform laws, called for a boycott of goods made by convict labor, demanded repeal of the contract labor law, urged international labor unity and pledged to help women workers and Negroes.

In 1868, only a year before his death, William Sylvis was elected president of the N.L.U. A thinker far ahead of his time, he pressed the federation to join the International Working-men's Association, commonly known as the First International, which had been formed in London in 1864 by Karl Marx and others. In arguing for international labor cooperation, Sylvis declared with a missionary's zeal:

"I have long been convinced of the beneficial results which would accrue to the interest of labor by an alliance with trade organizations throughout the world. Our aims, objects and interests are the same everywhere . . . and such unity would destroy the power of the capitalists to supplant workingmen struggling for their rights in one portion of the world by the importation of help from another . . . Our cause is a common one! It is a war between poverty and wealth; labor occupies the same low condition and capital is the same tyrant in all parts of the world . . ."

The N.L.U. sent a delegate to the convention of the International Workingmen's Association (I.W.A.) convention held at Basel, Switzerland, in 1869. The N.L.U. representative was loudly cheered when he told the Europeans: "My presence here . . . is an evidence that your friends in the New World recognize a common interest existing between the sons of labor the world over . . . I hope that my visit will be the first of many between American and European workers . . ."

In the short time he had left to live, Sylvis spoke out for the rights of female workers. Most unions barred women from membership and Sylvis called on them to drop the barriers. "How can we hope to reach the social levels for which we aim without making women workers the companion of our advancement? They deserve equal pay for equal work! It is only just and humane . . ." he said.

Pressed by Sylvis, the N.L.U. adopted a program which sought for women workers the same benefits as for men: the 8-hour day and an equal pay scale for equal work. The federation even had women delegates in its conventions, and appointed Kate Mullaney, president of the Collar Laundry Working Women's Union of Troy, New York, assistant secretary of the N.L.U.

Sylvis also tried to break down the color line in the unions belonging to the N.L.U. But here he ran up against hard-core resistance. White workers stubbornly refused to regard the Negroes as equals.

The Negroes, only recently emancipated from slavery, found that freedom was not the blissful state they had believed it to be. Thrown upon the labor market, the former slaves soon learned that their new "freedom" was a delusion. Employers hired Negroes at lower wages than whites received for the same work. In most factories only unskilled work was open to Negroes

79

although many of the ex-slaves had been carpenters, shoemakers, tailors, blacksmiths and mechanics. They were as well-trained and capable as whites; however, their wage scale was far below that paid other workers.

Without the protection of a union, isolated and discriminated against by both employers and workers, the Negro, even the most highly skilled, was forced to take any job at any price or else starve. In freedom, he existed on the same miserable level he had known while enslaved. Blind prejudice, bigotry, intolerance and fear caused white workers to hate Negroes. The idea of working with former slaves whom they considered "inferior" sparked much of the resentment and animosity displayed by the white men.

Sylvis begged the N.L.U. unions to accept Negroes. "The line of demarcation is between robbers and robbed . . . Capital is no respector of persons . . . it is impossible to degrade one class of laborers without degrading all . . ." he said in a speech at an N.L.U. convention.

But his words went unheeded. Instead of listening to Sylvis, the N.L.U. passed a resolution advising the Negroes to form their own national union which could send delegates to N.L.U. conventions. This was a timid step taken at a time when bold strides were needed.

Once the Negroes realized there was nothing for them in the N.L.U., they formed an organization in 1869. This new group, the National Colored Union (N.C.U.) went beyond putting forward economic demands. It tackled the social, political and economic problems of the Negro people and set forth demands, such as a special Homestead Act for Southern Negroes; free educational opportunities regardless of race; and full civil rights which would ensure Negro equality under the law, if not in fact.

Isaac Meyers, a former slave, was the first president of the N.C.U. He was a man much like William Sylvis, dedicated, self-sacrificing and courageous. Meyers traveled through the South to organize Negroes and whites; he did not believe in barring white men from the N.C.U. "There is no place for organizations based on the color of a man's skin," he said. "We are uniting in the interest of working men, black and white . . ."

Meyers met some success. He led a few victorious strikes and won concessions for his followers; but on the whole, the N.C.U. failed to achieve its primary purpose—the establishment of strong, permanent unions which any worker might join.

Nevertheless, the N.C.U. left its mark on the labor movement. This was the pioneer effort of Negroes to attain full recognition as citizens and workers; and by its mere existence the N.C.U. underscored the need of all workers to unite in the struggle for industrial democracy. It had not survived because white workers had forced the Negroes into a separate organization. This was stressed by an editorial in the *Boston Evening Voice*:

"If the workingmen have learned anything it is that there can be no hope of success but in union, the union of all labor . . . Labor cannot make any difference between black and white without undermining its own cause . . . The whole united power of labor is necessary to the successful resistance of the united power of capital . . ."

As the N.C.U. was failing, Sylvis was leading the N.L.U. onto an equally disastrous path. That undaunted leader became discouraged at the slowness of labor's progress and changed his tactics. He tried to revive the old producer-cooperatives of the 1840's. "The workers should own the businesses in which they work," he said. But that plan had misfired in the past and came to grief again for the same reason as before—the lack of money.

Sylvis then embarked on a program of monetary reform. The National Labor Union became the National Labor and Reform Party and came full tilt onto the political scene under the banner of the National Labor and Reform Party; but again, Negroes were excluded from membership. Unable to endorse the National Labor and Reform Party, the N.C.U., guided by its second president, the famed Frederick Douglass, backed the Republican Party which Douglass called "the true workingman's party of our country." Within a short time, the N.C.U. was completely absorbed by the Republicans.

Eventually, the National Labor and Reform Party went the way the Workingmen's Party had gone more than thirty years earlier. It could not withstand the harsh political blasts and disintegrated by 1872. Three years earlier Sylvis had died at the age of forty-one, a casualty of the war between capital and labor.

Although the National Labor and Reform Party was short-lived, it briefly made an impact in the United States. Once, the party's membership had totaled more than 600,000 and in 1868, Sylvis saw his brainchild hack out its one great triumph. That year, the party forced the passage of a law which brought Federal government employees the 8-hour day, a harbinger of the future, a beacon which kept alive the hopes of every worker.

The National Labor and Reform Party's fate proved one point; American labor, in the nineteenth century, could not win its ends by political action. The fight had to be carried on through militant trade unions. Shaken, but not whipped, American workers rolled up their sleeves and returned to the fray with clenched fists.

No one then knew that the next decade would be marked by hitherto unknown terror and violence as the war for men's rights raged more viciously than ever. Another era in the long history of the American labor movement was about to unfold.

Its trail was to be a bloody one.

workers striking for an 8-hour day, New York, 1872

2

The 1870's promised to be a decade of fabulous prosperity for the United States. It was a period of expanding business. A European visitor to America observed, "Any man with ambition, talent, luck and drive might well become a millionaire." If this somewhat exaggerated the situation, there certainly was truth to the fact that for the first time in the nation's history, wealth and affluence were attained by hundreds.

During the seventies in post-Civil War America, men lusted for money and did not care how they got it. Business ethics disappeared almost overnight. According to one writer, "The tactics employed by men of commerce would have shamed the pirates who once roved the Spanish Main . . . Business interests use fair means or foul. Men resort to trickery, bribery, corruption, thievery and even murder to gain their ends . . . Honor and decency are forgotten in the furious drive for quick wealth . . ."

In that hectic era, industrial and financial anarchy convulsed the country. Undisciplined and uncontrolled speculation took place. Men poured money recklessly into mines, factories, railroads and other enterprises; wildcat schemes flourished. Many projects were sheer gambles which had no chance for success. But this did not stop greedy speculators who plunged headlong, playing for the highest stakes. "Caution has become an ugly word. I do not know whither this money craze will lead us," a conservative New York banker wrote in 1871.

His answer came soon enough.

On September 18, 1873, the bombshell went off. The important banking firm of Jay Cooke, a noted financier, plummeted into bankruptcy. Cooke had dabbled unwisely in railroad construction and silver mining, suffering losses so huge that his bank's wobbly financial structure collapsed like a straw house in a tornado. Cooke's downfall set off a chain reaction. Many smaller banks that had been dependent upon him had to shut their doors. Panic spread like a smallpox epidemic. Fortunes were lost as one business after another failed. By the end of 1873, the country faced the worst economic crisis of its history.

The depression that followed the so-called Panic of '73, lasted seven dreadful years. The 1870's proved to be a decade of want rather than one of plenty. Human despair and misery ravaged the nation on a scale previously unmatched. Past panics and depressions dwindled into insignificance when compared to this disaster. The great and the small, the rich and the poor, were caught in the stranglehold.

Within an astonishingly short time over 4,000,000 men and women were jobless. In a nation of some 38,000,000 such unemployment amounted to chaos. The suffering among those without work was bitter. Thousands had neither food nor shelter; children starved and in cities from New York to San Francisco people roamed the streets "scrabbling in garbage heaps for a scrap of food or a piece of bread," according to one newspaper.

Massive demonstrations were held in city squares by the unemployed—drab, threadbare, pinch-faced throngs of desperate men and women and wizened children.

On January 13, 1874, more than 50,000 persons gathered in New York City's Tompkins Square to hear union leaders and labor officials speak. Present in the crowd was a young cigar

maker named Samuel Gompers who would one day win renown in the labor movement.

The meeting started peacefully with police on foot and horseback ringing the demonstrators. Although A. Oakey Hall, New York's mayor, had granted permission for the meeting, the police were on hand in force due to a rumor that anarchists were scheduled to address the assemblage. Without warning and for no apparent reason, a police captain suddenly gave orders to clear the square.

The police charged with clubs swinging; a troop of mounted men bore down on the crowd at full gallop. In moments, pandemonium broke out. Men, women and children were clubbed or trampled underfoot. Screaming and shouting, the terror-stricken people fled; scores were injured. Gompers, who took

Tompkins Square protest, New York, 1874

shelter in a nearby cellar, watched the ugly scene with dismay.

The cruel treatment meted out to New York's unemployed was repeated in city after city. The authorities reacted illogically in the face of rising discontent among the jobless. A Cleveland city official claimed the unrest stemmed from "foreign agitators" who wanted to overthrow the government and "replace Old Glory with the red flag of anarchy." Those in charge failed to understand that the disorders came as a result of empty stomachs and not the incitement of "agitators."

As unemployment rose higher, industrialists seized upon the situation to cut wages and "stamp out the insidious unions." The workers responded with resentment. Those still employed fought desperately to stave off wage reductions. From 1873 to 1880, the average worker's paycheck had been slashed almost

50 per cent. Jay Gould, the railroad magnate, when warned that further pay cuts might start a revolution replied, "I can hire one half of the working class to kill the other half."

Many strikes broke out, almost all marred by violence. Unrest reached its peak in the coal mines and on the railroads. Conditions in the minefields in eastern Pennsylvania were unbearably oppressive. The miners, mainly Irish immigrants, received miserable wages, were forced to live in company-owned shacks and had to trade in company stores at exorbitant prices. Almost every miner was in debt to the company for rent and food which came out of his wages. Often, a man worked all week and received only 50 cents in cash, the rest of his pay being deducted for food, clothing or rent.

In addition, the Irish suffered discrimination at the hands of foremen and mine officials, usually Welshmen or Englishmen who bore ancient political and religious grudges against Irishmen. From time to time the miners, loosely organized in a group known as the "Molly Maguires," struck back at their tormentors. From time to time a mine superintendent was waylaid and beaten, or a coal shaft dynamited. But these acts were the work of individual hotheads blindly hitting out in anger. Very few miners engaged in such practices or belonged to the Mollies.

In 1874–75, the so-called Long Strike paralyzed the coal fields. The operators decided to break the walkout by destroying the miners' union—the Workingmen's Benevolent Association. At the time the leading union smasher was Allan Pinkerton, who had headed the U.S. Secret Service during the Civil War and was now running a detective agency that specialized in "industrial protection." This meant he supplied employers with armed guards, strikebreakers, goons and labor spies.

Called in by the mineowners, Pinkerton offered the services of his foremost agent, James McParlan, who was Irish, Catholic and an accomplished labor spy with a long record of "union busting." McParlan, using the alias James McKenna, came to the coal fields. He joined not only the Workingmen's Benevolent Association, but also a secret society, the Ancient Order of Hibernians (A.O.H.), a fraternal social organization with branches all over the United States, to which most Irish miners belonged.

Franklin B. Gowen, a lawyer and president of the Philadelphia and Reading Railroad, operator of the mines, was eager to link the terroristic Molly Maguires with the A.O.H. and the W.B.A. If he could connect the three organizations and show the Mollies to be responsible for terrorism in the coal fields, Gowen believed the union could be broken.

Pinkerton's spy, McParlan, was ordered to find evidence which would show this tie-in. His opportunity came during the course of the Long Strike, when desperate miners resorted to violence. As the strike wore on, several mine foremen were shot, but neither the union nor the A.O.H. had anything to do with these crimes, although the perpetrators belonged to the organizations.

McParlan tracked down and exposed the killers who came to trial in 1875. Dubious evidence by unreliable witnesses "established" the fact that the criminals were not only Molly Maguires but A.O.H. and W.B.A. members as well. This gave Gowen, who prosecuted the case, the chance he had been seeking. Union leaders and militant miners were rounded up and accused of helping the murderers. In a mass trial twenty-four defendants were found guilty; ten received the death penalty and the rest were sentenced to long jail terms.

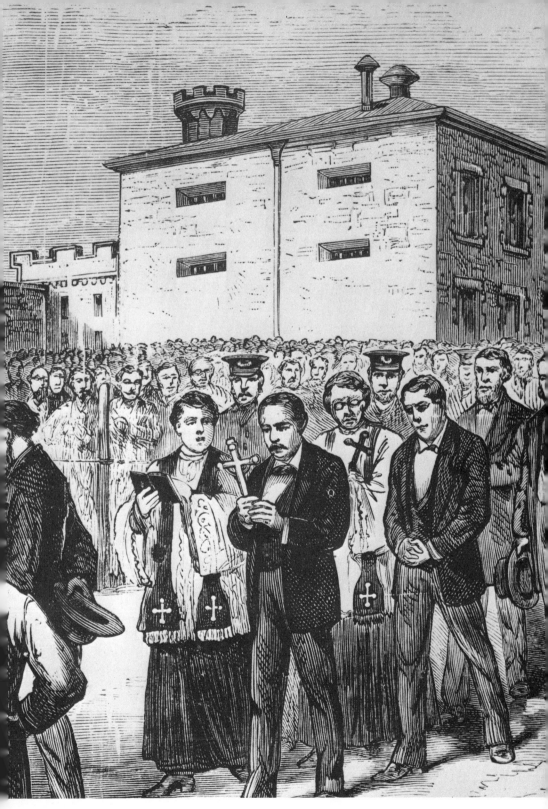

execution of the "murderous Molly Maguires," Pennsylvania, 1877

Branded as "murderous Molly Maguires," the condemned men died on the gallows and the executions were hailed by the nation's press as "true justice for black-hearted killers." A few liberal journalists noted that among the executed men were several whose only crime appeared to have been militant unionism. (Modern historians, after careful research, have expressed doubts that the Molly Maguires ever were very active in the coal fields; in fact, some even disclaim the existence of the group.)

The Molly Maguire hangings broke the strike. The men went back to work and a restive peace returned to the mines. The Ancient Order of Hibernians disappeared in the coal regions and the Workingmen's Benevolent Association was ground into the dust. For several decades afterwards any attempt to organize the miners was besmirched as "Molly Maguirism." The specter of the ten hanged men gave ample warning that the same fate awaited anyone who dared defy the coal companies.

The mineowners made doubly certain their workers remained passive by recruiting a private army called the Coal and Iron Police. This was a heavily-armed, well-paid corps made up of men who would not hesitate to use whip, club or gun on miners who protested the oppression under which they lived and labored. The coal operators' victory was a triumphant combination of legal and physical terror against a union.

The country had hardly recovered from the coal strike, when trouble broke out on the railroads. Since the onset of the depression in September, 1873, railroad companies had slashed wages by 25 per cent although during the same period, stockholders had received a dividend of eight per cent. On July 17, 1877, the Baltimore and Ohio Railroad (B & O) announced a 10 per cent wage cut for its brakemen and firemen.

The new wage cut enraged the workers. That same afternoon a train crew walked off the job in Maryland. Other men spontaneously stopped work throughout the Baltimore and Ohio system. The line was soon paralyzed. As the news became known about the situation on the B & O, workers on other lines also walked out. Before long, the Pennsylvania, New York Central and Erie Railroads were at a standstill. Without either pre-arrangement or plan, the B & O men had started a nationwide rail stoppage.

Railroad officials were frantic. Nothing like this ever had happened before. Telegrams bombarded state capitals demanding protection of railroad property. State authorities, most of whom had accepted graft from railroad magnates, hastened to satisfy their benefactors. First to respond was the Governor of Virginia who rushed militia to Martinsburg, where strikers had congregated at the railyard. The troops attempted to disperse the workers and fighting broke out. A rifle went off into the crowd and a striker was killed. Then a volley rang out, causing more casualties.

The townspeople and farmers of Martinsburg rallied to aid the strikers; they attacked the soldiers, tore up railroad tracks, burned rolling stock and slashed telegraph lines. Resentment, harbored against the railroads for years, broke forth in a violent convulsion.

The strike gained momentum and spread up the Atlantic Coast to New York, Pittsburgh and Boston; then the stoppage turned westward to Chicago, St. Louis and San Francisco. Militia was called out to guard the railroads and many battles flared between troops and strikers. The death toll soared. In some localities, however, militiamen refused to shoot at their fellow townsmen and in some places, joined the picket lines.

fighting in Baltimore during the Great Strike, 1877

Since they could not wholly depend on militia units, the railroad owners asked for Federal troops which President Rutherford B. Hayes promptly supplied. This inflamed the outraged public even further. Americans had been suffering from the worst depression in living memory. Hunger was everywhere and the poverty-stricken masses were infuriated at the sight of U.S. Regulars marching through the streets of their cities to defend millionaire railroad owners. In Baltimore, Pittsburgh, Chicago, St. Louis and San Francisco, thousands turned out to demonstrate against the soldiers.

"We Want Bread Not Bayonets!" the mobs cried.

But they received bullets and bayonets, not bread. The Regulars callously fired on the crowds. In Baltimore, an officer told his men, "The order is shoot to kill! Those people are mutinous rabble, scurvy anarchists who deserve a bullet! I want them shot without mercy!"

His men obeyed to the letter.

Ten strikers were killed by army bullets. That blood-drenched July, over 100 persons were shot dead and more than 300 wounded by U.S. troops. This stern repression broke the strike, but its memory lingered on.

The hard feelings engendered in July, 1877, did not quickly evaporate. The use of Federal troops against the strikers ended the long reign of the Republican Party for it lost the Presidential election of 1878. The strike also revived labor's participation in politics. The Greenback Labor Party was formed. It elected fifteen Congressmen and won many local offices.

The strike, which stirred the masses into action, also whipped the capitalists to a frenzy. The employers prepared for the worst amid growing fears that a revolution was brewing. Breaking the railroad strike did not give them sufficient comfort. Although they had beaten the trainmen, the industrialists were well aware that the conditions which had caused the upheaval on the railroads still existed. The situation was ripe for similar outbreaks.

A national magazine wrote:

"It will not do to be caught again as the uprising at Martinsburg caught us . . . We must meet force with force, and not permit a situation where a few thousand of the lowest type of laborers can suspend, even for a single day, the traffic of a great nation, merely as a means of extorting ten or twenty cents a day more wages from their employers . . ."

Local and state officials jumped to aid the frightened industrialists. Before long, fortress-like armories went up in many cities all over the country. Rifles, pistols, cannon and sabers were kept at hand and militia units stood ready for swift mobilization. Companies hired "special police" and armed guards recruited from the underworld. These steps enabled the employers to breathe a bit easier and gave them some assurance that any labor unrest would be dealt with harshly.

The lines of conflict were drawn more sharply than ever.

On the evening of December 6, 1869, eight years before the railroad strike, nine Philadelphia tailors had held a secret meeting in a dingy meeting hall. They were members of the local Garment Cutters Association, a union that had collapsed when it ran out of funds. The nine earnest tailors had gathered to talk over forming a new organization.

Their chief spokesman, Uriah S. Stephens, was a one-time Baptist minister and former schoolmaster. A tall, handsome man, Stephens had a flair for speech-making. He told his listeners that the time was ripe for "the complete emancipation of the workers from the thralldom of wage slavery . . ." To accomplish this he asked them to create a union founded on "universal brotherhood." In the past, Stephens argued, craft unions had failed because ". . . they were too narrow in their ideas and few of them looked far beyond a year . . ."

On the other hand he had vision and peered into the future. He foresaw "an organization of working people that will one day girdle the globe . . . It will include men of every craft, creed and color; it will cover every race worth saving . . ."

This grandiose dream was never realized, but at that meeting in Philadelphia the nine tailors formed the Noble and Holy Order of the Knights of Labor. The ranks of the Knights were open to every worker, or former worker, skilled or unskilled, male or female, white or Negro. The only persons excluded were those "who sell or make their living by the sale of intoxicating drink . . . and lawyers, doctors or bankers . . ."

Because of employers' black lists, anti-union sentiment and supra-legal action taken against trade unionists, the Knights of Labor (K. of L.) operated in elaborate secrecy. Stephens was determined to protect his followers from persecution. For that reason, the Knights of Labor adopted the clandestine rigamarole of fraternal societies such as the Masons, Elks, Knights of Pythias and Odd Fellows.

There were passwords, special handgrips, involved rituals, codes and cyphers, to pass on communications. Leading K. of L. officers bore high-sounding titles such as "Grand Master Workman" and "Venerable Sage." When a meeting was to be held the symbol was chalked on walls, fences, store fronts and house gates. The time and place for the conclave was given in cryptic symbols. Members never referred to the Knights by name, but called their organization "Five Stars." Despite this cloak-and-dagger rigamarole, the Knights grew from nine original members to almost 50,000 in ten years.

The K. of L. came out openly in 1879 on a national scale, with local "assemblies" in most cities. The Knights's slogan was "An injury to one is the concern of all," meaning that every worker had an obligation to another no matter what "his category of work, color, creed or sex . . ."

In 1879, three years before his death at the age of sixty-one, Uriah Stephens relinquished his post as Grand Master Workman and was succeeded by Terence V. Powderly, a thirty-year-old Irish Catholic.

Powderly had done many things in his lifetime. At sixteen, he went to work tending switches in the railyard at Carbondale,

Pennsylvania. A year later he was apprenticed to a machinist and by twenty was a full-fledged journeyman on the Delaware and Western Railroad at Scranton, Pennsylvania. But Powderly did not hold that job long. He quit to study law, managed a grocery store, served a term as labor mayor of Scranton and then became the K. of L.'s Grand Master Workman.

Slender and undersized with mild blue eyes that peered through silver-framed glasses, Powderly seemed an unlikely choice for a labor leader. "He reminds one of a harassed book-keeper, a sort of Bob Cratchit eternally abused by Ebenezer Scrooge," was one journalist's description of him.

However, Powderly's personality belied his appearance. There was little meekness, timidity or humility in him. A dynamic speaker with great persuasive powers, he had a talent for swaying audiences and was quite vain about his oratorical abilities. He had definite ideas about the purposes of a labor organization and how to better the workingman's condition. As had others before him, Powderly wanted to uplift the worker from his "lowly status" onto a higher social plane. A vague idealist, he sensed there was something wrong with an economic system that dragged thousands upon thousands down into poverty and inflicted on them the miseries of unemployment.

He felt that his life's mission was to "ameliorate the workers' lot" by bringing about "changes in the social order." Exactly what changes Powderly proposed were unclear. At various times he advocated all the shopworn remedies—producer cooperatives, land reforms and monetary reforms. One thing was clear, the Grand Master Workman hated conflict; he shied away from a fight and where his words were militant, his actions did not back them up.

Powderly detested strikes; he felt that they failed to bring the workers lasting benefits and sought other means of settling management-labor disputes. Although he stirringly declared that the laborer should "reap the fruits of his toil," he also insisted ". . . we mean no conflict with legitimate enterprise, no antagonism to necessary capital . . . I shudder at the thought of a strike . . ."

Under his leadership, the K. of L. came out for a cooperative society which would "benefit the whole people." He never fully defined this concept except to say that the masses must be educated for its advent.

In the ranks of the Knights were men grown restive; they had fought hard and long for better conditions and demanded action rather than sweet talk of a rosy future when "capital and labor would lie down side by side like the wolf and the lamb," as one worker stated it.

The Knights lustily sang:

"Storm the fort, ye knights of labor,
Battle for your cause:
Equal rights for every neighbor
Down with tyrant laws."

But with Powderly holding a tight rein on them, the Knights did little "storming" except with words. The Grand Master Workman tried to still the clamor of his followers for action on such concrete demands as an 8-hour day, higher wages, an end to child labor and other issues. When workers in many trades began talking of strikes, Powderly said:

"You have grown eager and anxious . . . Longing for results, you have overlooked the fact that full and complete preparations have not yet been made . . . To attempt to carry out our ideals in a week . . . a year or a decade would be folly . . . No hasty or ill-advised actions must be taken . . ."

To this a labor paper editor replied:

"It is well to be prepared. No good general leads an army into battle without making ready . . . but it is not necessary for the last button to be sewn on the last private's overcoat . . . Our Grand Master Workman has the roar of a lion and the courage of a lamb . . ."

Despite its shortcomings, the Knights of Labor gained in numbers. For the first time Negroes were welcomed without reservation into any labor organization. The Knights's credo that "an injury to one is an injury to all" was sincerely being practiced.

But good intentions were not enough. In 1884, another depression rocked the United States. This economic setback was neither as severe nor of such long duration as that of 1873–1880; the worst was over by the end of 1885. But the industrialists tried to use the unhappy situation to carry out wholesale wage slashing. By then, hundreds of thousands of persons belonged to the Knights of Labor; never before had there been so many organized workers. Local leaders felt the time had come for a show of strength. A number of militant strikes broke out.

Even though Powderly "deplored" strikes, he had to go along with the rank-and-file and lend support to these spontaneous struggles. The workers' offensive met with success and many strikes were victorious. The most signal triumph of the Knights came in 1885 against the Wabash Railroad.

The line's management had arbitrarily dismissed some K. of L. shopworkers. In retaliation the Knights ordered its members to boycott any work connected with the Wabash. This

"first annual picnic of the Knights of Labor—1882—
a cartoon by Joseph Keppler

would have disrupted operations on Jay Gould's Union Pacific Railroad.

Because Gould was anxious to avoid a railroad uprising such as had taken place in 1877, he persuaded the Wabash Railroad to reinstate the dismissed workers and grant all demands by the Knights of Labor on wages, hours and working conditions. It was a tremendous victory for the Knights; the frightened industrialists had attributed to the organization far greater power than it actually possessed.

An 1885 *New York Sun* article expressed the awe in which the Knights of Labor were then held. According to the newspaper:

> "Five men in this country control 500,000 workingmen and can at any moment stay the nimble touch of almost every telegraph operator; shut up most of the mills and factories and disable the railroads . . . These men compose the executive board of the Knights of Labor . . ."

Actually the *Sun* exaggerated, for even at the peak strength of 700,000 which it reached in 1886, the Knights never wielded such absolute power. But the organization did control large elements of the working class and its influence was widely felt in the United States; surely, no man then believed that 1886 would see the decline and fall of the Knights.

That crucial year brought change to the American labor movement, marking the ascendancy of a powerful new labor federation, and after seventeen years, new leaders rose to guide the workers through the struggles ahead.

In 1886, one sensed a turbulent spirit throughout the United States. Across the land people were dissatisfied. Men wanted more leisure, more time to enjoy life. The 8-hour day was still a burning issue.

On January 1, 1886, a numerically weak labor group, the Federation of Organized Trades and Labor Unions, which had been formed in 1881 by disgruntled craft unions who felt the Knights of Labor were not militant enough, issued a call for a nation-wide general strike on May 1, 1886, to make "the eight hour working day a reality." The idea stirred the minds and hearts of American workers. About 600,000 of them rushed to join the Knights of Labor in the mistaken belief that the country's best-known labor group would assume leadership of the 8-hour general strike.

Many of the new Knights were not aware that Terence Powderly opposed the strike call. He denounced direct action and spoke about a future society which would one day be achieved through "the united efforts of all who toil." He urged the workers to strive for a "just and humane society" rather than leading them head-on to win the 8-hour day.

Those thousands who flocked to the Knights cared little about what Powderly said. They planned to back the May 1 strike and when May Day came, walked off the job in vast numbers. Never before had the United States seen such a demonstration of labor solidarity. The strike shocked and alarmed employers in every major city and made them more determined than ever to crush the upsurging labor movement. They searched frantically for some weapon to use against the workers. In Chicago they found it.

Over 60,000 workers of the "Windy City" downed their tools on May 1. This wide response to the strike call worried Chicago's industrialists and political bosses. Something had to be done quickly or the union tide might spread to the stockyards, the heart of Chicago's economy. The meat packers would not stand for any work stoppage and word was passed to the police to crack down on 8-hour-day demonstrators. Soon nightsticks were breaking heads; marchers were arrested; peaceful parades became riotous free-for-all battles.

The management of the McCormick Harvester Works which employed hundreds of mechanics, had taken a drastic step to throttle the 8-hour-day talk in the plant. Early in February, 1,000 union men had been locked out and replaced by scabs. Several hundred Pinkerton detectives and strong-arm goons were hired to "protect" the plant and company property. The union workers turned the lockout into a strike. They joined the May 1 movement and celebrated when the massive demonstration brought an eight-hour day to over 200,000 men and women in various parts of the country.

On May 3, two days after labor's greatest single offensive, a mass rally was held outside the McCormick Harvester Works. August Spies, a Chicago anarchist and labor leader, was among those who addressed the meeting. As his speech was reaching an impassioned climax in which he called upon the McCormick workers to hold firm, promising that their solidarity would soon bring them victory, the plant's gates swung open. Out charged scabs, Pinkertons and goons to attack the throng. In moments, bricks, rocks and fists were flying. A platoon of Chicago police dashed up with drawn revolvers. Someone yelled "Open fire!" A fusillade crackled. When the gunsmoke cleared, six union men were dead and twenty wounded.

This bloodthirsty violence aroused hot anger in Chicago's working-class districts. August Spies wrote an inflammatory leaflet which was headed WORKERS! TO ARMS! TAKE REVENGE!

Other circulars, less emotional in tone, called upon the city's working people to assemble in Haymarket Square the following night at seven-thirty and voice their protest against the shootings at the McCormick plant. More than 3,000 men, women and children jammed the square to hear speakers denounce the police, the company and city officials. The crowd was surrounded by a strong police detachment numbering almost 200 men under the command of a Captain Bonfield.

Among the onlookers was Carter Henry Harrison, the mayor of Chicago. His Honor listened to the oratory of the well known anarchists August Spies, Samuel Fielden and Albert Parsons. The mayor noted that the dreaded radicals sounded "pretty tame." "They seemed more pink than red to me," he later stated. He also remarked that the meeting was proceeding in an orderly manner and there was not even a hint of violence, although the audience was noisily partisan.

About 9:30 P.M., a cold rain began to fall. The crowd, its ardor dampened, started breaking up and Mayor Harrison departed at 10 P.M. He went to police headquarters where he told the inspector-in-charge, "Nothing is going to happen in Haymarket Square, it will soon be over. I think the police detail can be recalled."

The rain quickly reduced the audience to only 500 persons. At 10:15 P.M., Fielden, the evening's last speaker was on the stand, making his concluding remarks. All at once, Captain Bonfield, whose men were drawn up behind him, loudly shouted, "I order you to disperse peacefully or take the consequences!"

Fielden stopped and smiled down from the platform. "Why, Captain, we are peaceable," he said. "Surely—"

He never finished the sentence.

A roar and a flash shattered the night. There were screams and shouts. Someone had thrown a bomb. The blast, which killed a police sergeant, was followed by shots as the officers fired point-blank into the crowd. Armed workers returned the fire. (It was not unusual for ordinary citizens to carry pistols in the Chicago of 1886.) When the shooting ended, seven policemen and four demonstrators were dead and possibly 200 people were wounded that night. The exact number of casualties could never be determined, nor was the person who threw the bomb ever found.

Press, police and industrialists blamed the anarchists. A mass hysteria gripped the public as headlines screamed about red terror, anarchist plots and foreign-inspired conspiracies. A lynch spirit pervaded the country. The Chicago police arrested the anarchists Samuel Fielden, Michael Schwab, Oscar Neebe, Albert Parsons, August Spies, Adolph Fischer, George Engel and Louis Lingg for the crime. No proof was offered that they had provoked the bomb throwing responsible for the deaths that resulted. The accused admittedly were anarchists and that was enough.

Before the trial a court official said, "It's as certain as death that those fellows will be hanged. The jury is packed. You can

Haymarket Square riot, Chicago, 1886

bet your bottom dollar that they'll swing." Seldom in American jurisprudence was a trial conducted with such animus. The newspapers daily called for a verdict of guilty. Hostile demonstrations against the defendants broke out in open court. The outcome was obvious from the start. Fielden, Neebe and Schwab received life sentences. Parsons, Spies, Fischer, Engel and Lingg were doomed to die on the gallows.

Of his fate, Fielden said: "I have loved my fellow man as I have loved myself. I have hated trickery, dishonesty and injustice . . ."

On the gallows, Fischer defiantly cried: "The more the believers in just causes are persecuted, the quicker will their ideas be realized."

Moments before he was hanged, August Spies declared, "There will come a time when our silence will be more powerful than the voices you are strangling today!"

As the hanged men were borne to their graves, 25,000 persons followed the coffins and 250,000 workers lined the route. According to the *New York World:* "There ran a feeling that the dead men . . . were martyrs in the cause of the poor against the rich, the weak against the powerful . . ."

Only one voice was raised in defense of the anarchists—a vehement voice, that of John P. Altgeld, who was elected governor of Illinois a few years after the trial. Declaring the "Haymarket Martyrs" innocent, he called the proceedings under which they had been sentenced "legal murder" and pardoned the three imprisoned men. This almost ruined Altgeld's political career but as a man of high courage and principles, he could not have done otherwise than correct such a "travesty of justice."

In the end, the Haymarket incident doomed the Knights of Labor. More than 200,000 members quit when they saw that the organization was not able to fight "labor's oppressors." The mighty champion of the underdog had failed in its severest test.

All the gains won by labor disappeared in the vicious reaction of a fierce anti-union campaign launched by the industrialists. By the end of 1887, the K. of L. ceased to be an effective organization.

But, like a phoenix, the American Federation of Labor rose out of the ashes and a new era of unionism came into being.

Samuel Gompers, the son of a Dutch-Jewish cigar maker, was thirteen years old in 1863 when his family migrated from London to New York. Young Gompers found employment as a cigar maker's apprentice. Twenty-three years later, he became a dominant figure in the American labor movement, heading the American Federation of Labor (A.F. of L.) from its inception at Columbus, Ohio, on December 8, 1886, until he died in 1924.

The A.F. of L. differed sharply from the defunct Knights of Labor, both in spirit and principle. Where the Knights had offered panaceas to the working class, such as land and monetary reforms and cooperatives, the A.F. of L. rejected what was termed "uplift" unionism.

"We're not do-gooders, reformers, salvationists or bleeding hearts," an A.F. of L. organizer said. "We don't give a damn about anything except making a good living."

Unlike the Knights, the A.F. of L. did not accept all who "worked for wages." It opened no doors to Negroes, women or unskilled workers, but limited its membership to skilled workers organized in craft unions and aimed to "protect the skilled trades from being reduced to beggary." Where the K. of L. had believed that " an injury to one is the concern of all," the A.F. of L.'s sole concern was the protection of skilled workers only. The craft unionists were determined to get the best conditions "by negotiation if possible, by direct action if necessary."

The A.F. of L. fostered an "aristocracy of labor," although industrialization and large-scale production were daily creating hordes of workers who lacked special talents. One day the craft unions would desperately need the support of those they formerly had shunned, but the A.F. of L. founding fathers did not look that far ahead. They catered only to the immediate needs of their members. To them, skilled and unskilled workers had nothing in common.

One of Gompers' closest aides, Adolph Strasser of the Cigar Makers' Union, bluntly summed up the A.F. of L.'s basic aims when he told a senatorial committee: "We have no ultimate ends. We are going on from day to day. We are fighting only for immediate objects—objects that can be realized in a few years."

The architects of the new federation, Samuel Gompers and Adolph Strasser of the Cigar Makers' and P. J. McGuire of the Carpenters' Union were hard-headed men, not visionaries; they did not dream, as had Powderly and Sylvis, of some vague future when capital and labor would live in peace and harmony. Although all three men once had been socialists, they long since had rejected the revolutionary aspects of that movement. Fully aware that a bitter conflict existed between worker and boss, Gompers, Strasser and McGuire had no intentions of wasting energy by trying to overthrow the established economic system.

In describing the attitude of the A.F. of L. leaders, one historian wrote: "They were content to continue in a master and servant relationship with capital, but wanted a bigger share as servants. Their motto was 'a fair day's wage for a fair day's work' and the ante rose higher all the time . . ."

An A.F. of L. union chief expressed it a bit more succinctly.

"We don't want pie in the sky! We want it now! And we want as big a hunk of it as we can get!"

Samuel Gompers was exactly the man to lead a cause with such a philosophy. He respected only skilled workers. The unskilled he described as "the albatross around labor's neck." In his youth he had worked side by side with cigar makers in dingy shops for little pay. Joining the Cigar Makers' Union, Gompers fought for better conditions in the industry. Later, he would often say, "I have not risen from the ranks! I am proud to be in the ranks."

Gompers hated nothing more than being "tarred with the brush of radicalism" and bent every effort to make the A.F. of L. appear respectable to business interests and the general public. He was pleased to win acceptance in high industrial and political circles.

In fact, Gompers had not always detested radicals. In the cigar factories he had met many socialists and other left-wingers. "New York was the haven for overzealous soldiers in the European struggle for freedom . . . They were men of imagination, courage, ideals. They sought their ends through revolution . . ." he wrote in his autobiography, *Seventy Years of Life and Labor*.

What turned him from a friend into a foe of left-wingers, was the fact that most Americans regarded socialists as "foreigners." Gompers became convinced that "foreign" radicals hampered the labor movement. Eventually he joined the clamor against the very men he once had described as possessing "imagination, courage and ideals." "Revolutionists are not the type that readily adapt themselves to the customs of a new land . . ." he said.

116

Recalling the Tompkins Square demonstration of ragged, hungry, unemployed workers he had seen broken up by the police back in the 1870's, Gompers remarked: "It was their own fault . . . They had acted in a way to make decent people turn against them. That mob had in it men and women who wanted to overthrow the government. There is no place within or outside the labor movement for those who would undermine the foundations of American democracy . . ."

When the A.F. of L. was formed, Gompers and his associates resolved that it would be a strictly "American" organization, untainted by radicalism. In Gompers' words, the Federation became "the business organization of the workers . . ."

In a short time Gompers showed that he was a highly talented executive. Under his guidance, the A.F. of L. soon stood on sound financial footing. He had seen too many examples of unions failing because they lacked funds to weather such emergencies as strikes and depressions. For that reason the initiation fees and dues were high in A.F. of L. unions; they rapidly accumulated sizeable reserves out of which could come money to pay strike, unemployment, sickness, disability and death benefits.

This was a new sort of unionism in keeping with the fast-stepping capitalist system. Gompers went even further. Formerly, union officers and organizers had been volunteers who worked on a hit-or-miss part-time basis. In the A.F. of L. this was not the case. Union officials were full-time, paid employees who ran the organization efficiently.

Business agents handled the affairs of individual unions. These shrewd and capable men kept a local's records, negotiated its contracts, handled disputes with employers and administered strikes, boycotts and membership meetings. Locals no longer were badly run but operated as smoothly as successful corporations.

Many business agents became expert negotiators who could win concessions for workers by bargaining with employers. Although the A.F. of L. did not shun strikes as an "ultimate" weapon, the unions preferred negotiating to striking. But, in the words of a business agent, "If we couldn't soft-soap them, we'd belt them in the jaw. Our boys would walk off the job in a minute, if I gave the word."

Gompers had his own theory about strikes: "The stronger the unions," he said, "the fewer the strikes. We do not want strikes, but if men are not well organized they will have to strike."

Some A.F. of L. business agents were unscrupulous, forerunners of modern labor "racketeers." They would accept bribes from employers to negotiate agreements more favorable to the bosses than to the workers; a few received payment as "insurance" against strikes; occasionally, an official absconded with a local's treasury. The majority, however, were sincere, hardworking, wholeheartedly seeking to win all they could for their members.

Because A.F. of L. unions served only the "aristocracy of labor" and not all workers, locals often operated undemocratically; a few officials sought to perpetuate themselves in office through "rigged" elections or by "roughing up" opponents. While this practice was not typical, it occurred on a scale previously unknown in the labor movement but neither had unions ever grown to such strength and importance as did those in the A.F. of L.

Since it followed a policy of having no "ultimate aims,"

the A.F. of L. did not venture into the political arena. Gompers made it a point to avoid politics although the Federation adopted a system of "rewarding friends" and "punishing enemies" at the polls. In other words, candidates favorable to labor received the unions' support. Others were denied the votes of union members. It was a program the A.F. of L. followed for nearly half a century. And during all that long period, the Federation patently ignored the thousands of unskilled workers. They had to wait until another day before anyone again paid attention to them.

As the nineteenth century was drawing to a close, American corporations grew to astounding proportions. In oil, steel, coal, sugar and railroads, corporate heads wielded almost despotic power. They had acquired wealth beyond imagination. Such tycoons controlled cities, states, whole regions of the country.

The corporations merged into monopolistic trusts which wiped out competition and raked in staggering profits. It was a time of stark economic greed. No one ever had dreamed businessmen could become so dominant in a democracy. But the "Barons of Industry" literally ruled the nation. President Grover Cleveland, who was no radical, once said:

> "Corporations which should be carefully restrained creatures of the law, and the servants of the people, are fast becoming the people's masters . . ."

The situation had reached a stage so abusive by the 1890's that a Federal investigation was launched to ascertain the effect of corporate influence on American life. One economist found the nation's wealth entrenched in the hands of a few dynasties: "Seven-eighths of the families hold but one-eighth of the wealth . . . while one per cent of the families owns more than the remaining ninety-nine per cent . . ." he reported.

Such blatant inequality brought bitter public reaction against "trusts" and "powerful business interests." Mounting protest forced Congress to pass the Sherman Anti-Trust Act in 1890. This legislation provided that "Every contract, combination in the form of trust or otherwise, or conspiracy in restraint of trade or commerce among the several states or with foreign nations is hereby declared to be illegal." However, the new ordinance had numerous loopholes. Things went on much as before.

Opposition to trusts took many forms. In Nebraska, where farmers were being victimized by exorbitant freight rates, trust-controlled farm machinery prices and high bank interest charges, a positive step was taken to curb the "Big Money" men. The farmers organized the Populist Party to elect local candidates.

"There are three great crops raised in Nebraska. One is a crop of corn, one is a crop of freight rates, and one a crop of interest. One is produced by farmers who by sweat and toil farm the land. The other two are produced by men who sit in their offices and behind bank counters and farm the farmers," wryly noted a Populist leader. "We intend to stop the farming of farmers!"

By 1892, the Populists had entered the lists on a national scale as the movement, which had sprouted in Nebraska, took root throughout the Middle West, the South and the Far West. Scores of Populists gained local office. Widespread support for the party came from factory workers, as well as farmers.

The best spokesman for the Populist Party was William Jennings Bryan, the "Boy Orator of the Platte," a Nebraskan, also called "The Great Commoner." Nominally a Democrat, Bryan had wrested control of that party from Big Business. In the 1896 Presidential campaign he ran against Republican William McKinley. Bryan's program was essentially that of the Populists. It included free coinage of both silver and gold at a ratio of 16 to 1, reviving again the perennial cure-all of the past

—money reform. The "Boy Orator" also called for the government to run the railroads and other public utilities as it did the post office.

The Republicans strove mightily to defeat Bryan; trusts rallied behind McKinley, pouring huge sums into his campaign. Standard Oil alone contributed $250,000, while meat packing firms donated $450,000 with equal sums coming from railroad, sugar and steel barons. Despite this enormous financial backing, McKinley barely nosed out Bryan, winning by only 600,000 votes. The Populist workers and farmers could not quite beat the "Robber Barons."

Historians blame Bryan's defeat on the A.F. of L. which adopted a "hands off" policy toward the election. Gompers was unwilling to risk a firm stand for Bryan. "He simply wouldn't stick his neck out," a union organizer noted. "Sam wanted to play on both sides at the same time. If he'd come out foursquare for Bryan, he'd have had Big Business sore at him and he just couldn't take that."

By 1896, Gompers should have known that no matter how labor catered to the capitalists, their crusade to destroy all unions would never slacken. He should also have learned that his failure to organize the unskilled workers was crippling the labor movement's fight to win higher standards for the American workingman. The self-styled "aristocrats of labor" in the A.F. of L. would suffer many bitter defeats because they lacked the strength to fight Big Business without the militant aid of the unorganized.

The most disastrous setback to Gompers' style of unionism came in 1892. In July, the Amalgamated Association of Iron, Steel and Tin Workers, an A.F. of L. union with 25,000 skilled members, sought to renew its contract with the Carnegie Steel Company, a giant corporation which produced most of the nation's steel. Back in 1889, the great steel magnate Andrew Carnegie had signed a three-year pact with the Amalgamated; the union wanted to negotiate a new agreement before the old one expired.

However, in July, 1892, Carnegie embarked on a European tour and company business was being conducted by Henry Clay Frick, the steel corporation's newly appointed general manager. Frick was a union hater. As owner of a coal mine, he had shown himself to be shrewd and ruthless in dealing with his workers. When Frick's employees had tried to organize, he overwhelmed them with scabs, Pinkerton men, Coal and Iron Police, and hired thugs.

Frick was determined to break the union at the Carnegie Company's main plant in Homestead, Pennsylvania. Even before the Amalgamated contract ran out, Frick ordered a high wooden fence crowned with barbed wire built around the plant. Rifle slits were cut in the wall and sentry boxes placed at its four corners. The workers dubbed the wall Fort Frick.

On July 6, two days before the contract was to end, the manager announced a wage cut to be immediately effective. This brought vehement protests from the steel workers who held a demonstration climaxed by the burning of Frick in effigy. Frick used this "rowdiness" as an excuse to shut down the mill in a "protective measure" and locked out all workers, union and non-union alike. In this way Frick declared war against the Amalgamated Iron, Steel and Tin Workers.

Although only 800 of the locked-out employees belonged to the union, 3,000 unskilled workers vowed to support them even if the mill reopened. Frick had anticipated this solidarity and sent to Pittsburgh for 300 Pinkerton "detectives" to guard the strikebreakers he intended hiring.

The Pinkertons, armed with Winchester rifles, left Pittsburgh after dark for Homestead, six and a half miles away. They traveled on two barges towed by a tug up the Monongahela River and reached Homestead at about 4 A.M. on July 7.

Union pickets, however, had spotted the approaching barges and as the detested Pinkertons started to land, alarm bells awakened the town. Men, women and children rushed to the dock, shouting, hooting and cursing the detectives. Flaring pine torches cast an eerie light over the scene. Suddenly, a shot rang out, then another. Someone in the crowd on shore screamed. Both sides opened up with rifles, shotguns and pistols; muzzle flashes stabbed the darkness.

A full-scale battle raged almost thirteen hours. The Pinkertons fought from the barges, holding out until the steel workers poured oil on the river and set it afire. Threatened by flames, the guards surrendered. The Pinkertons stumbled ashore amidst a barrage of rocks and sticks. They were hustled to the town hall and held there until placed in the custody of the county sheriff who escorted them back to Pittsburgh.

Seven workers and three Pinkertons were killed during the Battle of Homestead with an unknown number wounded. The clash was a temporary triumph for the strikers. Frick's hired army had been routed; the scabs had failed to come in and the furnaces of the Homestead plant went cold. Pickets marched jubilantly around Fort Frick but their joy was short-lived.

On July 12, 8,000 troops of the Pennsylvania National Guard, their bayonets glinting in the sun, entered Homestead and took over the town. The officer commanding the contingent

Homestead Strike, Pennsylvania, 1892

declared: "We are here to restore law and order." With martial law proclaimed, the strikers had to stand helplessly by while Frick imported more than 2,000 scabs to operate the plant under militia protection.

Despite the odds against them—eviction from company homes, hunger, sickness and the numbing knowledge that scabs had taken their jobs—the strikers held firm until November. Only then, with bleak winter on them, did the workers' ranks crumble. The unskilled, who had no stake in a union victory, finally returned to work on Frick's terms. The strike was broken. Soon after, at a meeting attended by only 200 of the Amalgamated's 800 members, the beaten men voted to go back.

Frick sent an exultant cable to Andrew Carnegie in Europe: "Our victory is now complete and most gratifying. I do not think we will ever have serious labor trouble again . . . We had to teach our employees a lesson and we have taught them one that they will never forget."

To this, Carnegie responded: "Life is worth living again . . . Congratulate all around . . ."

(Frick had himself been a strike casualty. On July 23, Alexander Berkman, an anarchist, broke into his office and assaulted him with knife and revolver. Only slightly wounded, Frick soon recovered; Berkman was arrested and sentenced to twenty-one years in prison.)

The debacle at Homestead wrecked the union. The steel industry was not again to be effectively unionized for more than forty years. During those weary decades steel workers lived on the edge of poverty. Skilled workers' wages fell almost 40 per cent; the rest slaved for only 16½ cents an hour. Homestead was a classic example of industrial ruthlessness as practiced by an American corporation in the 1890's.

Frick abolished the 8-hour day in Homestead immediately following the strike. Two 12-hour shifts kept the plant going full blast all day, every day. The Carnegie Steel Company prospered as never before in its history. During the seventeen years prior to the strike it had amassed profits totaling $27,000,000. But in the nine years after the struggle, the company's profits soared to $106,000,000.

The union's defeat had even more significance to the labor movement. It gave clear proof that the strongest craft union could not withstand the onslaught of a great corporation.

Somehow this logic escaped Samuel Gompers. The A.F. of L. continued on the same path for many years and the majority of the nation's workers had to live in economic misery because the Federation's leaders stubbornly refused to recognize that craft unionism was an outmoded concept.

Not every labor leader clung to craft unionism as tenaciously as did Samuel Gompers. There were many who saw the weaknesses in the A.F. of L. but did nothing about remedying them. One man, however, did. His name was Eugene Victor Debs, born November 5, 1855, in Terre Haute, Indiana, of French immigrant parents. At the age of fourteen, Debs was working in the railway yards of his home town.

Ardently interested in unionism, Debs became secretary-treasurer of the Brotherhood of Locomotive Firemen by the time he was twenty-five. As he gained experience in the labor movement, Debs began to realize that craft unions had outlived their usefulness. That sort of labor organization could not keep up with the rapid development of industry.

"A modern plant," Debs said, "has a hundred trades and parts of trades represented in its force. To have these workers parcelled out to a hundred unions is to divide and not organize them . . . The dominant craft should control the union . . . and it should embrace the entire working force. This is the industrial plan, the modern method applied to modern conditions, and it will in time prevail . . ."

The discontent he felt toward craft unionism grew stronger and reached its peak in 1893 when several railroad brotherhoods refused to support a strike led by the Switchmen's Union. This convinced Debs that "craft chaos does not serve the worker." He resigned from the Brotherhood of Locomotive Firemen and with several other leaders formed a new organization, the American Railway Union (A.R.U.), built along industrial lines and taking in all railroad workers. Debs was elected president of the union.

Before the A.R.U. celebrated its first birthday, Debs and his followers were hit by the strongest attack yet hurled against organized labor. The small town of Pullman, just outside Chicago, was the battleground. Owned by the Pullman Palace Car Company, which employed about 5,000 workers in its various shops, steel mills, factories and foundries, the town had been established as a model community by George Pullman, the company's founder.

In the words of a company official, Pullman was a town "where all that is ugly and discordant and demoralizing is eliminated, and all that inspires to self-respect is generously provided." These were high-sounding words, but they fell flat on the ears of the workers who had to live there. The company owned the houses their employees lived in; it owned the stores, the library, the church, even the water and gas supply. The residents of Pullman had to buy at the company stores; they had to live in its houses and they paid whatever rates the company demanded.

"You liked it or you lumped it," a Pullman employee said. "We had no choice; and we took what was dished out because in those days, jobs were hard to come by . . ."

The company collected for rent, groceries and all other services by deducting the sums from employees' pay checks. According to the minister of the Pullman Methodist-Episcopal Church, one man had left after deductions, "a paycheck of two cents . . . he never cashed it, preferring to keep it framed, as a memento . . ."

Although the Pullman Company had existed only twenty-seven years in 1894, its stockholders received an annual dividend of eight per cent. There was a depression in 1893, but that did not affect the Pullman yearly dividend. In fact, the company announced a surplus of $4,006,488—the highest ever. Despite banner business, Pullman slashed employees' wages from 25 to 40 per cent between September, 1893, and May, 1894. Company living costs, however, remained at the same levels. The workers simply could not get along on their reduced salaries; men found only $1 to $6 in their pay envelopes for two weeks' work.

Finally the workers decided to take action. They formed a grievance committee to meet with George Pullman, but the company head told them, "We have nothing to talk about." The next day three of the committeemen were fired.

This was too much. On June 21, 1894, the Pullman workers voted to strike. (During the preceding months, some 4,000 of them had joined Debs's A.R.U.) For several weeks, Debs vainly tried to arbitrate with company officials. Pullman stubbornly refused to deal with the union. At last Debs lost patience. He ordered members of the A.R.U. not to handle Pullman cars anywhere in the United States. On every railroad from coast to coast, switchmen detached Pullman cars from trains and scores of A.R.U. men were discharged. In response to this, Debs called a general rail strike. Within a few days nearly every railroad in the country was at a standstill.

The strike was almost 100 per cent effective. Freight piled up in warehouses; only a few passenger trains rolled. The American Railway Union, despite its youth, showed a strength never possessed by any craft union; under fire industrial unionization proved itself an effective labor weapon. For some days a union victory seemed certain, but the railroad magnates were not yet defeated.

The General Managers' Association, a group made up of twenty-four railroad companies stood solidly behind the Pullman Company against the union. The Association opened a shattering counter-offensive. Scabs were taken on to replace the strikers.

The railroad operators next called upon Attorney General Richard Olney for special deputies to prevent the "obstruction of cars bearing U.S. mail." Olney complied by swearing in some 3,600 "special deputies" who were armed with clubs and guns and sent out to patrol the railroad lines around Chicago. The General Managers' Association footed the bill for these men. It came to more than $400,000.

A newspaper reporter noted that most of the deputies ". . . appeared to be of a type that never before had been on the right side of the law . . . Every drinking den, beer hall and pool room in Chicago must have been emptied of its boozers, loungers and loafers to fill the ranks of that bunch . . ."

The legalized thugs provoked many incidents with the strikers, particularly in the Chicago area. As violence rose, Illinois Governor John P. Altgeld mobilized the state militia; under his firm direction the guardsmen would have put down further disturbances. However, the General Managers' Association, aware of Altgeld's sympathy toward labor, was not satisfied with the Illinois militia. The railroad operators appealed to President Grover Cleveland for Federal troops.

The President complied, rushing four companies of the 15th U.S. Infantry to Chicago. The arrival of regular army troops evoked a protest from Altgeld. In a telegram to the President, he said:

". . . you have ordered Federal troops to go into service in the State of Illinois. Surely the facts have not been correctly presented to you in this case or you would have not taken this step, for it is entirely unnecessary, and, it seems to me, unjustifiable . . . The local authorities have been able to handle the situation . . . The Federal government has been applied to by men who had political and selfish motives for wanting to ignore the state government . . ."

Cleveland curtly told Altgeld that he had sent the troops to make certain that the U.S. mail was unhindered.

"The fat was in the fire once the soldiers came," wrote a *New York World* reporter. "Nothing in the world could then have prevented bloodshed . . ."

The strikers resented the army being used to protect the scabs who manned mail trains which were also used to haul freight and passengers. Resentment turned into hostility. Some strikers stoned a detail of soldiers and fighting broke out.

Rifles cracked and bayonets flashed. Chicago was torn by near civil war as workers fought troops. During the course of the conflict army bullets and bayonets killed thirty strikers and wounded scores. But the strike remained solid despite the "blue-bellies"—an 1894 slang term for U.S. soldiers.

According to an Associated Press dispatch from Chicago, ". . . the strike inaugurated by the American Railway Union holds most of the railroads running through this point in its strong fetters . . . Neither soldiers, martial law, bullet or bayonet can break the will of these determined union men . . ."

The railroad bosses realized that something more drastic than force had to be used against the A.R.U. The General Manager's Association resorted to the courts for help.

132

"King Debs"—1894—a cartoon by W. A. Rogers

It came quickly on July 2 in the form of an injunction issued by Federal Judge Peter S. Grosscup. The court order named Debs, sixteen union leaders, and "all others" who sought to interfere with rail transportation, the U.S. mails and the "normal operation" of the twenty-four railroads involved in the strike.

133

Grosscup's injunction forbade every activity involved in conducting the strike including peaceful picketing by "all and sundry persons whomsoever . . ." Anyone who disobeyed the "blanket" order was subject to arrest and imprisonment for contempt of court.

Debs and fellow union officials refused to honor the order and urged their followers to ignore it. As a result, hundreds of strikers were jailed. Debs, of whom the eminent lawyer Clarence Darrow once had said: "There may have lived sometime, somewhere, a gentler more generous man than Eugene Debs, but I have not known him," was aroused to fighting pitch. He called upon all labor to support the A.R.U. in its "battle against tyranny."

A labor convention, with delegates from many unions, was to convene in Chicago for the purpose of declaring a general strike throughout the United States in sympathy with the A.R.U. But before action could be taken, Debs and several A.R.U. officers were arrested and imprisoned for six months on charges of violating the injunction.

Without leadership, the workers were unable to continue the struggle. Early in August, the strike fizzled out and defeated strikers straggled back to their jobs. The General Managers' Association and the Pullman Company emerged victorious. The loss of the strike doomed the American Railway Union.

From prison, Debs wrote, "I once believed that the American workers could redress their wrongs through industrial unionism. But in the glint of bayonets and the flash of rifles my eyes have been opened wide . . ."

The Pullman strike's outcome made Eugene Debs a militant socialist. For over three decades he was the leading light of the Socialist Party and ran as its Presidential candidate in

1900, 1904, 1908, 1912 and 1920. During the 1920 campaign, Debs was serving a jail term for having opposed America's entry into World War I. So strong was his appeal to the working class, that he polled almost 1,000,000 votes.

If the Pullman strike brought Debs to Socialism, it also taught the employers there was an easier way to break a strike than resorting to violence. The injunction, which a union official called a "Gatling Gun on paper," had proven far more effective than bullets, billy clubs and bayonets. By this tactic, industry could throttle labor without the adverse publicity the use of force provoked.

Small wonder that striking unions were literally buried in an avalanche of injunctions. Every time a strike was called, the employer secured a court order prohibiting the union from undertaking any measures to further the strike. On those rare occasions when a judge could find no grounds to issue an injunction, the bosses quickly reverted to the old methods of strikebreaking—scabs, clubs, guns and terror.

The Harvest Time

Since 1900

1

As the twentieth century dawned, strong winds were blowing in the labor movement. Their force was immediately felt in the coal fields of Pennsylvania where miners had been enduring cruel conditions since the ill-fated Long Strike of 1874–75 and the Molly Maguire hangings. Because the men were badly treated, poorly paid and forced to work in grave danger of sudden death from cave-ins or explosions, they had made numerous attempts to unionize.

By 1902, the United Mine Workers (U.M.W.) had signed up thousands of men. This militant union led by 28-year-old John Mitchell, who once had been a coal miner, finally mustered the strength to win a strike in the bituminous or "soft coal" fields of Pennsylvania, Ohio, Indiana and Michigan. The U.M.W. gained recognition plus concessions on wages, hours and safety regulations for the bituminous miners.

With that victory under his belt, Mitchell then led the U.M.W. into the anthracite or "hard coal" regions of Pennsylvania where the Molly Maguires had died and the Long Strike had been disastrously defeated twenty-five years earlier.

On May 9, 1902, Mitchell called his men out of the pits after fruitless negotiations with the coal operators. The mine-owners girded to break the strike with terror. The Coal and Iron Police force was mobilized and over 1,000 specials deputized. Scabs were gathered from all over the country; but few strikebreakers actually knew how to mine coal; many balked at going down into the mines.

Mitchell had cautioned his followers against violence. "The blood that will be spilled will be yours," he warned. Despite all kinds of provocation, the U.M.W. men obeyed him. The Coal and Iron Police and the specials could find no excuse to use guns and clubs. The strike dragged on for months. With each day, sympathy rose for the embattled coal miners. Mitchell's temperate leadership, his requests for an impartial committee to arbitrate the strike and the strikers' discipline impressed the public. On the other hand, the operators hurled wild charges of "anarchy" and revolutionists" at the United Mine Workers.

But words could not mine coal. As winter approached, an acute anthracite shortage threatened the United States. The nation's industries and plants were fueled by coal, the country's homes heated by it. Obviously something had to be done to break the deadlock.

President Theodore Roosevelt stepped in. He warned the operators that unless they sat down to negotiate with the U.M.W. the U.S. government intended sending troops to the coal fields, not as strikebreakers, but to seize the mines which would then be run under government supervision. For the first time, Federal authority was being used on the side of the workers and the voice of organized labor was heeded in high places.

The mineowners, faced with an irate President and an angry public, agreed to accept the recommendations of an arbitration commission appointed by Mr. Roosevelt. A mutually suitable settlement was made and the strikers returned

140

to work with banners flying. They had not won every demand, but the U.M.W. was firmly entrenched in the hard coal regions. At long last, the martyred Molly Maguires had been vindicated.

The victory in the anthracite mines was but a strong gust. The hurricane was yet to come. It blew out of the West with a mighty blast that rocked the nation.

On June 27, 1905, an extraordinary convention met in Chicago, attended by 186 delegates who represented more than a dozen unions ranging from "gandy dancers" (railroad track-walkers) to merchant seamen and brewery workers. At the meeting was a rough-and-tumble union officer, thirty-six-year-old William "Big Bill" Haywood, the treasurer of the Western Federation of Miners (W.F.M.). A stoop-shouldered, one-eyed giant of a man, Haywood had led a colorful life as a lumberjack, cowboy and miner in the copper, silver and lead mines of Colorado, Minnesota and Nevada.

Haywood's W.F.M. practiced a tough line of unionism. If mineowners hired thugs to raid union meetings, the W.F.M. retaliated by dynamiting a mine shaft. The raids would end abruptly and the hoodlums would be seen no more. Scabs, Pinkertons, company finks and goons, were met with fists, clubs and bullets.

"I never yet saw a scab who didn't have a yellow streak up his back . . . If you slug it out with him, toe-to-toe, you can bet your bottom dollar he'll take it on the lam," Haywood once said. "A working stiff has to fight or they'll make a doormat out of him."

With other W.F.M. officers, "Big Bill" believed that labor needed One Big Union; a single organization to which every workingman might belong regardless of his job. Miners and bakers, cooks and lumberjacks, carpenters and longshoremen, all united in One Big Union. And from the One Big Union would evolve the One Big Strike. Never again would workers wage lonely, isolated struggles. Every worker in the country—perhaps in the world—would be his ally, ready to strike if necessary. The One Big Union was a revolutionary idea, but it captured the imagination of many.

To find a sympathetic audience for his views, Big Bill Haywood went to Chicago as a W.F.M. delegate to the June meeting which had been called by radical unionists and left-wingers from all over the country. These were people grown impatient with the slow progress made by the American Federation of Labor; they were tired of Gompers and what they called the "American Separation of Labor." These fiery union men and women wanted immediate action and meant to get it.

It was an oddly assorted crew that had drifted to Chicago. Daniel De Leon, an inspired Socialist orator, stood with gentle Eugene Debs; black-bearded Father Thomas J. Hagerty, the editor of a Catholic labor newspaper, rubbed shoulders with a little gray-haired old lady, a veteran union fighter known as "Mother" Jones.

They had journeyed to Chicago, these dissidents, socialists, idealists, dreamers, anarchists, revolutionaries, reformers and crusaders, for the cause of human rights. The newspapers reviled them as "wild-eyed Reds" and "blood-thirsty radicals"; the Chicago police hounded them; hired detectives spied on them, but they remained undaunted.

The convention delegates proposed to form a new labor federation to combat the A.F. of L. When Samuel Gompers heard this, he sneered, "That bunch will fall apart. They'll never agree on anything." His prediction finally came true, but for about fifteen years, "that bunch" gave the "American Separation of Labor" a lesson in bold unionism and brought sleepless nights to many an employer.

Guided by De Leon, Debs and Haywood, the Chicago convention formed the Industrial Workers of the World (I.W.W.). The American labor movement never since has seen its equal. The I.W.W., popularly known as the "Wobblies," was founded on principles directly opposite to those of the A.F. of L. Where Gompers stood for business unionism, the Wobblies called for revolutionary unionism.

In a thundering preamble written by Father Hagerty, the I.W.W. proclaimed:

"The working class and the employing class have nothing in common. There can be no peace so long as hunger and want are found among millions of working people and the few, who make up the employing class have all the good things of life . . ."

The Wobblies rejected the A.F. of L. demand for "a fair day's wage for a fair day's work." Instead, they urged abolition of the wage system, stating in part:

"It is the historic mission of the working class to do away with capitalism . . . By organizing industrially we are forming the structure of the new society within the shell of the old . . ."

Further, the I.W.W. manifesto declared the workers ought to own and run "all means of production and distribution . . ." Once that occurred there was no need for workers to be "wage slaves" since they would own all the country's wealth.

143

The delegates who founded the I.W.W. were not merely prattling when they talked about One Big Union and One Big Strike. There were about a dozen basic industries in the United States at that time; if each was organized into One Big Union it would not be impractical to call the One Big Strike thus enabling the workers to seize control.

This was a revolutionary doctrine and the convention did not try to mask its purpose. At its final session, the assemblage rose and lustily sang "The International," shouting the closing lines:

"We have been naught,
We shall be all!"

The Wobbly credo set American workers afire with excitement. Soon men were discussing the I.W.W. in mines, mills, factories and fields. Lumberjacks, migratory farm workers, meat packers, seamen, factory hands, Negroes, foreigners, women, skilled and unskilled, all who had been neglected by the A. F. of L. flocked to the I.W.W.

The One Big Union reached out for the downtrodden. "We are going down into gutter to get at the mass of workers and bring them up to a decent plane of living," Big Bill Haywood said.

The Wobblies did that. Before long it was claimed that nearly 1,000,000 workers carried a "Red Card"—the color of the I.W.W. membership card. Perhaps time has distorted the size of the I.W.W., but it can never dim the impact the Wobblies made on the United States. They brought vigor, courage and color to the labor movement.

slogans and stickers of the I.W.W.

An I.W.W. organizer named Joe Hill was also a talented songwriter and composer; he turned his skill to creating songs with catchy tunes about labor's struggles. At the height of the I.W.W. movement Joe Hill's songs were sung around camp-fires in the harvest fields, on picket lines, at mass meetings and rallies, in workers' clubs, in demonstrations. There was scarcely a person in the United States who had not heard "Hallelujah, I'm a Bum!"—"That Rebel Girl"—"Mr. Block"—"They Go Wild Over Me"—and the favorite of all Hill's works, "Pie In The Sky."

In 1914 Joe Hill led a successful strike against a Utah construction company. Vengeful Salt Lake City authorities allegedly framed him on a murder charge. Hill was sentenced to death and executed by a firing squad in the Utah State Penitentiary despite a tremendous campaign by the Wobblies and other labor groups to save him. His last message to Bill Haywood was: "Don't mourn! Organize!"

Soon after he had helped found the I.W.W., Big Bill Haywood, along with Charles Moyer and George Pettibone, officials of the Western Federation of Miners, were accused of murdering Frank Steunenberg, a former governor of Idaho. Steunenberg had held office at a time when the W.F.M. was conducting a series of strikes in Idaho lead and silver mines. There had been much violence and the governor used stern measures against the miners. W.F.M. members harbored deep hatred of Steunenberg.

The ex-governor was blown to bits by a bomb and the Pinkerton Detective Agency took over the investigation of the slaying. One of the detectives on the case was James Mc-Parlan, the man who had destroyed the Molly Maguires more than a quarter of a century earlier. The years had not altered McParlan's techniques. He found a shady character named Harry Orchard, a W.F.M. member, who confessed to murdering Steunenberg, as well as twenty-six other enemies of the union.

According to Orchard, all the murders had been planned by the three W.F.M. leaders—Haywood, Moyer and Pettibone. The accused men were in Colorado at the time Orchard implicated them; but Idaho officials did not wait for extradition proceedings. They kidnapped Haywood, Moyer and Pettibone, and kept them in an Idaho jail for eighteen months until the trial began in 1907.

These high-handed tactics aroused widespread public indignation. The I.W.W., the Socialists and various other militants raised thousands of dollars for a defense fund. Clarence Darrow was hired as counsel for the imprisoned labor leaders. Darrow conducted a brilliant defense; he made mincemeat of Orchard's testimony. Even the biased Idaho jury had to render a "Not Guilty" verdict.

Bill Haywood was free to conduct the I.W.W. crusade. He led it with a broadsword. Incredibly energetic Wobbly organizers went about the country signing up workers in every industry. There were I.W.W.-led strikes in canneries and meat packing plants. Transport workers and window cleaners won gains under the I.W.W. banner. The Wobblies sparked big strikes and small ones. "We'll go wherever working stiffs need us," an I.W.W. organizer promised. And the Wobblies kept their word. They agitated among farmhands and in city streets, not only talking unionism, but also preaching socialism on street corners.

Authorities and employers detested the Wobblies. The I.W.W. was castigated as being made up of "bums" and "tramps." Newspapers called them the "I Won't Works." Wobbly organizers were jailed, tortured, beaten, killed; a mob in Oregon lynched several I.W.W. men. But terror did not daunt these working-class warriors. Any town where Wobblies were arrested for holding street meetings became the scene of a "Free Speech Fight."

Wobblies by the hundreds descended on a community and night after night men spoke on street corners. They read aloud the Declaration of Independence, the Bill of Rights or made radical speeches to provoke arrest. Soon local jails were packed with singing Wobblies. This continued until town officials could no longer afford to feed the prisoners and had no place to keep them locked up. The I.W.W. conducted scores of "Free Speech Fights" and won most of them.

The Wobblies did not hesitate to meet violence with violence. In McKees Rocks, Pennsylvania, where 8,000 workers of fourteen different nationalities struck against the Pressed Steel Car Company during 1909, the employers called on the state constabulary. This mounted force, known as the "Pennsylvania Cossacks," was noted for its brutality in labor strife. After a striker was shot, the strike committee warned that a Cossack would be killed for every worker "murdered or wounded." The constabulary abruptly ended the violence and the strike was quickly won.

The biggest victory gained by the I.W.W. was the 1912 Lawrence, Massachusetts, textile strike which involved 30,000 foreign-born employees of the American Woolen Company. The walkout came about spontaneously when the company

148

cut the already low wages of the workers, most of whom had been earning only $9 a week. With cries of "Short Pay! Short Pay!" loom operators, mostly young women, rushed out of the shops. They belonged to no union and had no leaders but knew that it was impossible to live on the pittance the company had handed out.

Two I.W.W. organizers, Joe Ettor and Arturo Giovannitti, rushed up from New York to give the strikers sorely needed guidance. Picket lines were established and soup kitchens set up. For those who understood no English, pamphlets and leaflets written in Russian, Polish, Lithuanian and Italian were distributed. The walkout lasted for weeks and weeks, bringing much suffering and hardship to the strikers.

The winter of 1912 was a bitter one and conditions grew so desperate that strikers' children were taken in by sympathizers of other towns and cities. On February 24, 1912, police attacked a group of youngsters and mothers about to board a train for Philadelphia. Women and children were clubbed mercilessly in this vicious attack. The brutal incident brought widespread support for the Lawrence strikers. Even the newspapers changed their attitude. Describing the assault on the wives and children of the strikers, a reporter wrote:

"It was a scene one would have expected in Tsarist Russia not the United States . . . I shall never forget the shrill screams of frightened children . . . nor the blood which crimsoned the snow . . ."

Within a few weeks the American Woolen Company capitulated and granted all the workers' demands. When the mills re-opened, the strikers returned with wage increases that ranged up to 25 per cent.

"Bell Time"—a painting by Winslow Homer

The I.W.W. led many more strikes. Some they won, some they lost, but each struggle was conducted with boldness and integrity. However, the organization was not destined to last long. Its fate was sealed in 1917 when America entered World War I. Haywood and ninety-six other Wobbly leaders denounced the conflict as an imperialistic war and refused to support the national war effort.

The government passed a series of laws aimed at suppressing anti-war groups. Wobblies were jailed by the thousands; socialists, such as Eugene Debs, were imprisoned. When Big Bill Haywood was sentenced to prison, along with a number of I.W.W. chiefs, the leaderless organization floundered and was all but destroyed. Haywood skipped bail and in 1921, fled to Russia where the Communist revolution had taken place four years earlier. Big Bill died in Moscow in 1928 and was buried with full honors in the Kremlin.

The savage repression of the I.W.W. went on even after World War I ended. The organization waned and became a shadow of what it once had been. But in their prime the Wobblies had seriously challenged the A.F. of L. and craft unionism. If nothing else, the I.W.W. showed that industrial unionism could work; it proved the value of the unskilled, the foreign-born, the Negroes and women formerly scorned by skilled workers.

And though the I.W.W. virtually disappeared from the labor scene, the ringing defiance of the old songs echoes out of the past. The present-day civil rights struggles smack of the "Free Speech Fights" of another time when brave men and women marched against democracy's enemies under the banner of the I.W.W.

In 1917, as the United States prepared to "make the world safe for democracy" in the "war to end all wars," Woodrow Wilson was the darling of organized labor. The scholarly President had spoken out for the workingman; he talked of "industrial democracy" and "economic freedom." By more than words, Wilson had shown himself to be labor's friend. During his first administration, in 1914, Congress had passed the Clayton Act. This law clearly stated labor unions were not "trusts" or combinations in restraint of trade as many employers claimed.

The Clayton Act declared:

"The labor of a human being is not a commodity or article of commerce. Nothing contained in the anti-trust laws shall be construed to forbid the existence and operation of labor organizations instituted for the purposes of mutual help . . . nor shall such organizations be held . . . illegal combinations or conspiracies in restraint of trade under the anti-trust laws . . ."

Gompers hailed the act as "the Magna Carta of Labor." Workers made other important advances under Woodrow Wilson. At the President's urging, Congress created, on March 4, 1913, a separate Department of Labor (until then there had been a Department of Commerce and Labor). The Secretary of Labor was made a member of the President's Cabinet. This action brought status and dignity to American labor.

153

In his inaugural address Wilson had called for a "New Freedom"—a society in which workers would enjoy decent living and working conditions with "rational and tolerable" hours of labor. Above all, the President emphasized that the nation's working people were entitled to have the freedom "to act in their own interest."

"The Man In The White House means we have the right to organize! We've been given the green light! Watch our smoke now!" an A.F. of L. official said.

Unparalleled union activity took place in mine, mill and factory. Workers flocked to join existing unions while new ones sprang up overnight. In the building trades almost 300,000 carpenters, masons, bricklayers and painters carried union cards. The United Mine Workers membership soared. In garment "sweatshops," where Jewish and Italian immigrants labored for pennies in dark and airless lofts, tailors, stitchers and cutters rose up against degrading industrial slavery.

On every side, labor was on the move backed by a humanitarian President who wanted to help the working people. Labor idolized the "Schoolmaster," as Wilson was known. Never before had prospects seemed brighter for American workers. Radiating optimism, Samuel Gompers said: "We are no longer in the season of planting; we are in harvest time."

The A.F. of L. chief erred. The great struggle was far from over. More than 90 per cent of the country's workers were unorganized. Non-union immigrant Poles, Russians, Hungarians and Italians toiled twelve hours a day at substandard wages in the steel mills. No unions existed in automobile, farm machinery, meat-packing plants, to name only a few major industries.

And no matter what the President said, Big Business still

154

opposed unionization. Had Gompers removed his rose-colored glasses he might have seen the real picture. America was far from a workers' paradise and labor still had to travel a steep, rocky road.

In 1917, the United States leaped gaily into the First World War with such enthusiasm that someone likened America's attitude toward war to that of undergraduates attending a big football game. The few Americans who raised objections to the conflict were quickly and effectively silenced. Samuel Gompers strongly endorsed President Wilson's war message of April, 1917. The A.F. of L. chief proclaimed: "This is labor's war!"

And at first most American workers agreed with him. Unions gave a no-strike pledge and raised the slogan, "Everything for the boys at the front!" Some workingmen shouldered rifles and sailed "Over There." The others, union and non-union alike, toiled hard to turn out the tools of war. Factories ran twenty-four hours a day.

But then came trouble. Living costs soared. The price of staples daily rose higher. Workingmen found they could not feed their families. While wages remained constant, prices did not. The workers protested the high cost of living and breaking their pledge, struck for more pay. Before the end of 1917, at least 1,000,000 persons were participating in 4,450 strikes.

Wilson ended this distressing situation by forming a War Labor Board which included union heads, employers and government officials. Both management and labor made concessions. Employers agreed to pay a "living wage . . . which will insure the subsistence of the worker and his family in health and reasonable comfort . . ."

The minimum wage for each industry was clearly stated

155

in every government contract. Unions were authorized to act as bargaining agents for workers. Women factory workers had to receive equal pay for equal work. In return for all this Gompers gave assurances that there would be no more strikes for the duration of the war.

On November 11, 1918, World War I ended. Shortly after, the 2,000,000 Yanks who had gone to France came home —except for the 126,000 dead at St. Mihiel and Chateau Thierry, in the Argonne Forest and the Ardennes. But the war was over and everyone wanted to forget the ordeal. "Let's get back to normal!" became a national slogan.

The A.F. of L. leaders wrongly concluded that the post-war years would be marked by industrial peace and that the gains labor had made during the war were permanent. Labor soon found out that its honeymoon days with management were over. Employers, big and small, could hardly wait until government controls were lifted. They had always resented Federal fixing of wages, hours and compulsory union recognition. For employers the end of the war also put an end to the enforced good will displayed toward labor.

"The hour of reckoning was at hand. I couldn't wait for the time when I'd be able to clean house, get rid of the union and run my business my way," a shoe manufacturer said. "We'd had enough of those busybodies in Washington telling us what to do and how to do it. I hated unions before the war, I hated them during the war and I still hate them. Now, I can do something about it."

His attitude prevailed in most industries. Employers felt the unions had been riding too high and needed to be knocked down. Workers were also in an aggressive mood. While the war was on, they had kept their bargain by not striking. But

156

with peace, living costs kept skyrocketing and every worker knew the tremendous war profits corporations had earned.

"We don't have to hold back any longer. There's no reason why we should scrimp to buy our kids milk while the bosses eat filet mignon," a union leader told his men. "It's time to rear back and demand our piece of the big war money. If we have to hit the picket line to get it—let's go!"

This attitude inevitably led to conflict. During 1919–1920, a strike wave inundated America. It was estimated that well over 1,000,000 workers marched on picket lines. Building trades workers, shoemakers, telephone operators, actors, steel workers and in Boston, policemen were on strike by mid-November 1919, only a year after the Armistice.

Consternation gripped the country; the strikes had come like a deluge and wails of fear rose from all sides. Only two years earlier the Communist (Bolshevik) Revolution had taken place in Russia; led by Nicolai Lenin and Leon Trotsky, the Reds had overthrown the capitalist system, and established what they called the "Dictatorship of the Proletariat"—a workers' and peasants' government.

By 1919, similar uprisings were taking place in several parts of Europe. These revolts always had been preceded by strikes; the same pattern seemed discernible in the United States. Perhaps the Bolshevik virus was infecting the U.S.A.! American employers charged that the strikes were led by "Bolsheviks" and "Communists"; that the unsettled labor situation was a "Red" plot. (The Boston police strike over demands no more radical than a small pay raise, evoked scare headlines: "The Bolsheviks Are Taking Over!")

As the so-called Red Scare mounted, U.S. Attorney General A. Mitchell Palmer initiated a widespread crackdown on radicals. His raiding parties seized hundreds of people, jailing some, deporting others. Despite Palmer's efforts, the strikes still continued. If Communists had anything to do with the work stoppages, their role was a minor one. As prices spiraled, workers simply needed more money in order to live—and this need was the principal cause of the 1919–1920 strike epidemic in the United States.

The biggest labor upheaval was a walkout at the United States Steel Corporation. Not since the Homestead strike of 1892 had the steel workers been unionized. The 1919 struggle was led by William Z. Foster, a one-time Wobbly, who then worked for the A.F. of L. (Gompers had shed his abhorrence of radicals in Foster's case. "That man's a crack organizer He can do the job in steel. We need him!" Gompers said.)

Foster justified the A.F. of L. chief's faith in him by signing up 100,000 steelworkers in Pittsburgh and other steel-producing centers. The workers labored under incredibly dismal conditions. They demanded better wages and an 8-hour, rather than a 12-hour day. Elbert Gary, head of the U.S. Steel Corporation, told a union negotiating committee, "Our corporation and its subsidiaries, although they do not combat labor unions as such, decline to discuss business with them."

The steel strike started September 22, 1919, and was crushed by January 9, 1920. Gary unleased unbridled force against the strikers: police, militia, Coal and Iron Police and Pennsylvania Cossacks. Pickets were clubbed, trampled and shot. The ruthless suppression was justified by the steel industry on the grounds that the strike heralded a general Communist insurrection.

The propaganda worked. Foster's radical past was disclosed. Besides, weren't the strikers a pack of "hunkies," "dagoes" and "niggers"? What difference did it make how that kind was treated? Such "trash" wanted to trample on the Flag and destroy the constitution. Down with the Reds!

So the steel workers were beaten, as were coal miners who struck at the same time. The Red menace had been stopped in its tracks!

3

In November, 1920, Warren G. Harding was elected President on the promise that he would bring "normalcy" to the country. By 1921, the United States had entered the period of Harding's "normalcy" and the "Roaring 20's," a decade of bootleg whiskey, raccoon coats, fast spending and freewheeling prosperity. Within a year, business improved, wages went up and the strikes had ended. Times became good. Nothing like it had ever been seen before anywhere in the world. Everybody was making money, doing fine. America was off on a grand spree. Under Harding, Uncle Sam no longer poked his nose into business, but left such matters to businessmen. Employment was at a record high; strikes were a relic of the past. This was prosperity.

By 1923, the A.F. of L. had lost its post-war militancy. After all, in such times, who wanted to talk about strikes or betterment of labor conditions? Nobody cared to stir up trouble. American workers owned cars, wore silk shirts and ate "high on the hog." Only fools, madmen or Reds would try to sabotage the well-oiled machinery of Harding's "normalcy."

A.F. of L. leaders silenced grumblers in the ranks by pointing out how well things were going for their members. Sure it was true that thousands of textile workers in the South were underpaid, that children labored in mills, that workers in rubber, auto and other basic industries remained unorganized. So what? Of course there were still sweatshops. Who cared?

160

This wasn't the time to upset the apple cart. Not when everything was going so swell!

"You can't have Utopia! This is the U.S.A., not the Garden of Eden. Most working people are satisfied. The rest are out of luck," a high A.F. of L. official said.

Organized labor grew soft and flabby during the 1920's. Samuel Gompers died in 1924, eulogized by both unions and employers as "The Grand Old Man of Labor." If there was some muttering against him among the rank-and-file, it went unheard in the speeches of praise. Gompers' place was taken by William Green, the son of Welsh immigrants, who had been an official of the United Mine Workers. A one-time coal miner, Green promised that he would adhere to the "fundamental principles of trade-unionism as championed by Mr. Gompers."

Some unions were taken over by gangsters and racketeers in the "Roaring '20's" as members lost interest in organizational affairs. In a few industries employers wooed workers from A.F. of L. unions by setting up "company" unions which were more concerned with management's welfare than the workers. Instead of better wages and working conditions, company unions provided such "fringe benefits" as picnics, bowling teams and outings.

As labor's militancy ebbed, corporations returned to union-busting tactics. They again circulated blacklists naming union "troublemakers." New employees had to sign "yellow dog" contracts which stipulated they would not join an outside union. Labor spies kept tabs on union activities in factories. Industrialists started a movement for the "open shop" which meant that both union and non-union men could be hired. It was called the "American Plan" implying that belonging to a union was somehow "un-American."

161

The strength and dignity of the trade unions was whittled away. A relatively few workers remained militant and retained the post-war fighting spirit.

During the lush 1920's the American working class stirred out of its lethargy only once. In May, 1920, two anarchist labor organizers, Bartolomeo Vanzetti and Nicola Sacco, were arrested in Braintree, Massachusetts, on a charge of murdering a paymaster during the holdup of a shoe factory in April.

The evidence against them was weak. Sympathizers claimed they were being tried for their beliefs rather than the crime. Sacco, a shoemaker, and Vanzetti, a fish-peddler, were found guilty and sentenced to death in the electric chair. Liberals, union men, left-wingers and intellectuals rallied to their cause. The case dragged on until August 22, 1927, when the men were electrocuted.

That night rioting and mass demonstrations rocked many cities of the United States and Europe. No man could ever forget Vanzetti's eloquent words written on the eve on his execution. He said, in part:

"If it had not been for this thing, I might have lived out my life talking on street corners to scorning men. Now we are not a failure . . . Our words—our pains—nothing! The taking of our lives—the lives of a good shoemaker and a poor fish-peddler—all! The last moment belongs to us—that agony is our triumph!"

Even as Vanzetti sat writing in his cell, no one could have known that a few years later millions of Americans would be suffering agony of a different sort—the demeaning torture of the Great Depression which would cast a black shadow on the next decade.

162

October 24, 1929, the stock market crashed and the day became known as "Black Thursday." The debacle in Wall Street triggered a depression unmatched in severity and duration.

By 1932, 14,000,000 Americans were unemployed; thousands lived in makeshift shacks along river banks, on the fringes of cities and in public parks. When the high-flying '20's came to their dismal end the United States was unready to face a cruel economic crisis. Within a brief span Americans tumbled from affluence to poverty.

Workless men shuffled on breadlines for a handout; war veterans in tattered uniforms sold apples on street corners; children wore patched and mended hand-me-downs; and in people's faces one could see only despair. Who could have believed that in mighty America hunger would stalk the streets? The nation was stunned, the government paralyzed. The people seethed with unrest and bitter frustration.

Huge demonstrations of unemployed marched in the cities. "We Want Jobs!" the masses shouted. But there were no jobs. Harried officials could offer only the degradation of a small "home relief" check, a few dollars which were not enough to live on.

The Federal government, under President Herbert Hoover, offered help to Big Business rather than the suffering unem-

163

ployed. Hoover's theory was that "prosperity at the top" would "trickle down to the bottom." But he was wrong; no matter how he tried to bolster business in 1930 and 1931, nothing did any good. Banks collapsed, shops closed and once-busy communities became ghost towns. Some cities even lacked funds to pay teachers, firemen and police. In the words of a newspaper columnist, "Uncle Sam has gone to the cleaners . . ."

The A.F. of L. was stunned by the depression. As industries shut down, the Federation lost whole locals at one swoop; with 14,000,000 workers jobless, the A.F. of L.'s membership dwindled alarmingly. However, there were union men still working and they fought hard against pay-cuts. Violent strikes broke out in various parts of the country.

In the 1932 Presidential campaign the people overwhelmingly repudiated Herbert Hoover and turned to a man who had promised to give the nation a "New Deal." Franklin Delano Roosevelt came into office at the blackest hour of the nation's history. America was demoralized, all but beaten on March 4, 1933, when Roosevelt delivered his inaugural address, a speech that galvanized the country.

"There is nothing to fear but fear itself," he declared. "A host of unemployed citizens face the grim problem of existence, and an equally great number toil with little return . . . Only a foolish optimist can deny the dark realities of the moment. Our great primary task is to put people to work . . ."

To this job, Roosevelt bent all his energies. A bewildering assortment of agencies were set up to initiate the New Deal. There was a Public Works Administration (PWA) that spent millions on building bridges, highways and public buildings to provide many jobs.

164

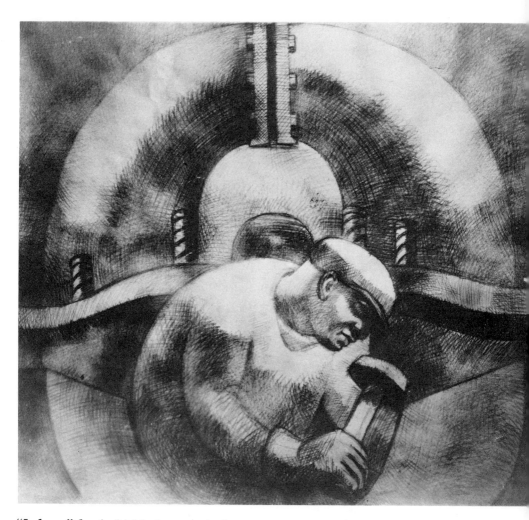

"Laborer" by A. Lishinsky—a painting commissioned by the W.P.A.

The PWA, at a later date, was taken over by the Works Projects Administration (WPA) which employed actors, writers, dancers, artists, musicians, teachers and professionals as well as skilled and unskilled workers. The Civilian Conservation Corps (CCC) gave work to many unemployed youths and helped with reforestation and conservation.

So many abbreviations appeared in the newspapers that a bewildered reader wrote to a newspaper editor, "It looks as though somebody upset a bowl of alphabet soup." Even the President was tagged with an abbreviation of his name. Franklin Delano Roosevelt became FDR.

The Chief Executive worked tirelessly to fulfill his promise to "put people to work . . ." As an aid to industry, he set up the National Industrial Recovery Act (NRA) to stimulate business through fair competition, curtailment of overproduction and regulated prices. The NRA also established minimum wages and hours codes. Its Section 7(a) gave workers the right to organize and bargain collectively without interference from employers.

This was a big boost for labor. A tremendous upsurge in unionism got underway. Banners saying "President Roosevelt wants you to join the union" appeared in the coal fields. In a short time about 1,500,000 workers had joined the A.F. of L.

But the initial outburst of enthusiasm soon waned. The Blue Eagle emblem of the NRA was derided as the "Blue Buzzard" by both industry and labor. Despite the codes' provisions, management refused to honor Section 7(a); indeed, corporations forced employees to join company unions. Labor was dissatisfied with the NRA, soon to be nicknamed the "National Run-Around," because the codes had no powers of enforcement.

Unionism was in the air, however, and the workers were willing to fight for the rights the government had so benignly bestowed. Strikes broke out in the rubber, auto and textile industries; union organizers braved the Ku-Klux-Klan (K.K.K.) and other terrorist organizations in the Deep South. The great port of San Francisco was paralyzed by a general strike in 1934.

Business as a whole fought the NRA and demanded a return to "free enterprise." As the depression's icy grip loosened, the clamor against the codes grew louder. At last, without regret from either management or labor, the Supreme Court declared the NRA unconstitutional. But labor continued to receive the government's protection. Eleven days before the death of the NRA, on June 5, 1935, the National Labor Relations Act, popularly known as the Wagner Act, named for Senator Robert F. Wagner of New York, was passed by Congress.

It fulfilled the promises of the NRA. By its provisions the Wagner Act prevented management from hiring labor spies, using blacklists, forcing workers to sign "yellow dog" contracts, establishing company unions, threatening workers for joining a union, discriminating against union men and refusing to negotiate with a union.

A shout of joy went up from labor circles; the Wagner Act was hailed as a second "Emancipation Proclamation." But the jubilation of the unions was matched by the fury of the employers. A desperate campaign was mounted against the Wagner Act. Nevertheless, the Supreme Court declared it a valid law on April 12, 1937, after two years of furious corporate resistance.

From 1935 on there were fierce and savage battles along the labor front. An investigation by a congressional committee revealed that 2,500 corporations employed the services of labor spies; one automobile corporation spent $830,000 for spies, scabs and munitions. A steel company had on its premises 8 machine guns, 369 rifles, 190 shotguns, 450 revolvers, 6,000 rounds of ammunition, 109 gas guns, 3,000 tear-gas shells.

An investigator exclaimed, "Good Lord, you have weapons enough for a small war!"

"That's right," a company official nodded grimly. "That's damned right! And we're ready to fight a war anytime the union wants to start one."

At the time the furor was being raised about the Wagner Act, the labor movement was undergoing an internal upheaval. John Llewellyn Lewis, head of the United Mine Workers, the son of a Welsh miner, had started to work in the pits when he was twelve, in his twenties he was a union organizer and finally he rose to the presidency of the U.M.W.

For years, Lewis had been advocating a shift from the traditional A.F. of L. craft unionism. He favored industrial unions and raised the issue on the floor of the A.F. of L. Convention in 1934 and again in 1935. Lewis had many supporters including outstanding labor leaders such as Sidney Hillman, Amalgamated Clothing Workers; David Dubinsky, International Ladies' Garment Workers' Union; Charles P. Howard, International Typographical Union; Max Zaritzky, Cap and Millinery Workers' International Union and others.

A hot feud broke out between Lewis and the Old Guard represented by William Green, William Hutcheson of the Carpenters Union, Daniel Tobin of the Teamsters, Matthew Woll of the Photoengravers and John P. Frey of the Metal Trades Union. These men clung tenaciously to craft unionism.

At last, in an effort to placate Lewis, the A.F. of L. allowed him to form a Committee for Industrial Organization within the framework of the Federation. But Green combatted every effort Lewis put forth. The A.F. of L.'s Old Guard hampered him as he tried to organize mass-production workers in steel, radio, automobile, rubber, textile and many other industries.

In 1937, the ten unions that formed the Committee for Industrial Organization were expelled from the A.F. of L. Green warned that they would be "exterminated." John L. Lewis scoffed, "I fear his threats as much as I believe his promises."

The Committee became the permanent Congress for Industrial Organization (C.I.O.) and the work of unionizing the unorganized went ahead full blast. Everywhere rose the cry "Join the C.I.O.!" Workers responded by hundreds of thousands. Before long 100,000 steel workers were signed up and U.S. Steel, the nation's largest corporation, quickly accepted the C.I.O. The chairman, Myron C. Taylor, admitted the futility of putting up a struggle against such a mammoth union. "This is not 1919," he said. "We must move with the times—and today, the trend is towards unionism."

But the second largest steel company, Republic Steel, refused to meet with the C.I.O. The corporation head, Thomas Girdler, was fanatically anti-union. He fought the Steel Workers' Organizing Committee under Philip Murray, a former colleague of John L. Lewis in the United Mine Workers. The strike that followed at Republic produced a tragedy. On Sunday, May 30, 1937—Memorial Day—striking workers held a picnic about a half mile from Republic Steel's South Chicago mill. They had been on strike for a week and the picnic took the form of a rally. The strikers who had brought their wives and children were having a fine holiday, when the peaceful assemblage was suddenly attacked by police and special deputies armed with guns, tear-gas grenades and axe handles.

Without any provocation a volley of shots rang out. Men

169

fell dead; women and children ran shrieking as more shots whistled past; the police charged, beating all within reach. The ugly incident gained infamy as the Memorial Day Massacre. Ten strikers were killed and many were wounded. That outburst of brutality broke the strike.

It was the C.I.O.'s first defeat, but the battle raged on in the auto industry. Members of the United Auto Workers' union struck the Fisher Body Plant in Flint, Michigan. They used a technique popular among French workers but then unknown in America. Instead of walking out, the men "sat down" inside the plant, a move that initiated a spate of sit-down strikes spanning the nation. Workers in industries ranging from rubber and glass plants to five-and-ten-cent stores used the sit-down.

The Supreme Court eventually declared this to be illegal; but by that time the sit-downs had attained results. In almost every case, the workers won. So the labor conflict flared throughout the late '30's and into the '40's. The strife between C.I.O. and A.F. of L. also continued until it was interrupted by a greater battle. On December 7, 1941, the Japanese bombed Pearl Harbor and the United States was caught up in World War II.

Both great labor organizations pledged to support the war effort and promised not to strike; it was a promise well kept except for a few wildcat strikes and one stoppage in the coal fields. Between December 7, 1941, and the end of the war, according to the U.S. Bureau of Labor Statistics, only $\frac{1}{100}$ of one per cent of scheduled working hours was lost through strikes.

The post-war years saw many clashes between management and labor; almost every major industry had strikes when workers

170

struck for higher pay to meet rising living costs as they had done in 1919. But it was different this time. Unions were powerful and well-financed; they were able to conduct long, drawn-out strikes and did so.

By 1946, the strike waves petered out with general increases for the workers. Many unions also set up health, welfare and retirement benefits for their workers. But the unions had grown so strong that a general feeling against them rose up. Unhappily, some unions became infested by underworld elements who had wormed their way into positions of top leadership.

As a result of growing anti-union sentiment in the United States, Congress passed the 1947 Taft-Hartley Act. A complex piece of legislation which limited to some extent the power of unions, the Act became law over President Harry S. Truman's veto. Among the Taft-Hartley Act's provisions was a clause which required union officials to swear they never had and did not currently belong to the Communist Party. Unions were forbidden to contribute to political parties; strikes could not be called without sixty days' notice; the closed shop was banned under a "right to work" proviso. Although the Act did not please labor, it did help to breach the differences between the C.I.O. and the A.F. of L.

Then on November 5, 1952, Philip Murray, who had succeeded John L. Lewis to the presidency of the C.I.O. in 1940, suddenly died of a heart attack. Twelve days later William Green, the A.F. of L.'s president for almost thirty years, also died. Walter Reuther, chief of the United Auto Workers, replaced Murray; George Meany was elected head of the A.F. of L.

These progressive, farsighted men, Meany and Reuther, finally managed to heal the wounds that had so long separated the two labor groups. On February 9, 1955, they merged and became the A.F. of L.-C.I.O. with a total membership of more than 15,000,000 working men and women. George Meany was elected head of the organization. The days of machine guns, clubs and tear gas were gone; there would be no more Homesteads, no more Memorial Day Massacres. A new vista had opened for labor; a new spirit of cooperation with management pervaded the unions.

Now the trade union has become an accepted fact in American life. And in the words of Walter Reuther, the aims of the American labor movement are to "gear economic abundance to human needs . . . we would like to show the great new world that can be built if free labor and free management and free government and free people can cooperate together in harnessing the power of America and gearing it to the needs of the people . . ."

The way has been difficult. The labor movement now faces new struggles and problems, but the trail to a better and more abundant life has been blazed.

It only remains to follow the path.

AUTHOR'S NOTE

I have attempted to tell the long and continuing story of the American Labor Movement. In a time when unions are both reviled and praised, I believe it is important for young readers to gain some understanding of their background.

It would have been impossible, in a book such as this, to detail all the complexities which marked the growth of trade unionism in America; that would take volumes. I have touched lightly, explored briefly and even skipped over certain phases of the saga; but if this book awakens some comprehension of the struggle for industrial democracy in America, my purpose is accomplished.

In modern times trade unionism has outgrown its colorful roots. Men seldom sing labor songs. The slogans of bygone days seem quaint and outmoded. Today it may require effort to realize that once there was vehement opposition to old-age pensions, unemployment insurance and the 40-hour week, or that men, women and children sometimes died violently to win an 8-hour-working day.

But all this happened.

By today's standards, the American worker is truly an "aristocrat of labor" when compared to his father or grandfather. However, every benefit now taken for granted had to be wrested from grudging hands.

If there is much violence in this book, it is because the American labor movement was bitterly contested every step of its arduous march. The fight for trade unionism in the United States has been marked by bloodshed and brutality; it is neither a pleasant nor a pretty story, but one that must be truthfully told.

I wish to thank all those who helped me with this book. I owe special debts to librarians at the New-York Historical Society, the New York Public Library and to certain private sources. I am grateful to Henry Chafetz and Sidney Solomon of the Pageant Book Company for providing me with invaluable research material.

Accolades are due my wife for putting up with my grouchiness, my young son for steering clear during working hours and Mrs. Lee Levin for typing the manuscript. As always, my agent, Miss Candida Donadio, was readily available with sage advice and good cheer.

I. W.

New York City
January, 1965

FURTHER READING

Adamic, Louis — *Dynamite: The Story of Class Violence in America.* Gloucester, Massachusetts: Peter Smith, 1959.

Austin, Aleine — *The Labor Story.* New York: Coward-McCann, 1949.

Bimba, Anthony — *The History of the American Working Class.* New York: International Publishers, 1937.

David, Henry — *The History of the Haymarket Affair.* New York: Collier Books, 1964.

Debs, Eugene V. — *The Writings and Speeches of Eugene V. Debs.* New York: Hermitage Press, 1948.

Foner, Philip S. — *History of the Labor Movement in the United States.* New York: International Publishers, 1947.

Gompers, Samuel — *Seventy Years of Life and Labor.* New York: E. P. Dutton, 1943.

Haywood, William — *Bill Haywood's Book.* New York: International Publishers, 1929.

Huberman, Leo — *The Labor Spy Racket.* New York: Modern Age Books, 1937.

Josephson, Matthew | *The Robber Barons.* New York: Harcourt, Brace & Co., 1934.

Kornbluh, Joyce L., Ed. | *Rebel Voices: An I. W. W. Anthology.* Ann Arbor: University of Michigan Press, 1964.

Oneal, James | *The Workers in American History.* New York: Rand School of Social Science, 1921.

Pelling, Henry | *American Labor.* Chicago: University of Chicago Press, 1960.

Powderly, Terence V. | *The Path I Trod.* New York: Columbia University Press, 1940.

Walsh, Raymond J. | *C.I.O.* New York: W. W. Norton and Co., 1937.

ABOUT THE AUTHOR

Irving Werstein is the author of many fine books which have particular meaning for young people today. His aim is to recreate dramatically and accurately a moment or a period in history; to uncover knowledge of past events that will help safeguard the future.

Mr. Werstein was born in Brooklyn, graduated from high school in Richmond Hill, Long Island, and attended New York University. He and his wife are enthusiastic travelers and have lived in Mexico, Italy, England, Denmark, France and Holland.

With their son Jack, the Wersteins now make their home in New York City.